Peter Erler
Hubertus Knabe

The Prohibited District

The Stasi Restricted Area Berlin-Hohenschönhausen

Edited by
Stiftung Gedenkstätte Berlin-Hohenschönhausen

Jaron Verlag

With the kind support of Stiftung zur Aufarbeitung der SED-Diktatur

1st Edition 2008

(Original title: „Der verbotene Stadtteil. Stasi-Sperrbezirk Berlin-Hohenschönhausen“)

www.jaron-verlag.de
Translation: Miriamne Fields, Berlin, and Marie Frohling, Berlin
Cover design: Atelier Kattner, Berlin, with use of a photo by Federal Commission for the Records of the State Security Service of the former German Democratic Republic
Map pgs. 6/7: Gedenkstätte Berlin-Hohenschönhausen
Layout: Prill Partners | producing, Berlin
Lithography: LVD GmbH, Berlin
Printed and bound by: Westermann Druck Zwickau

ISBN 978-3-89773-584-2

Contents

Introduction

It was terra incognita: Until 1990 parts of Bahnhofstrasse and Genslerstrasse, as well as the Freienwalder and the Lichtenauer Strasse, in the East Berlin district of Hohenschönhausen, were not indicated on any map of the city produced in the GDR. Only an empty space appeared in place of the actual street layout. On site, the ignorant passerby was confronted with closed metal gates, watchtowers and armed security personnel.

As of 1945 a secret, prohibited district was located within this highly guarded, restricted area that initially fell under the direction of the Soviet secret service, which later transferred it over to the GDR's State Security Service in 1951. The establishment and expansion of this institution lead to the destruction of a large part of Hohenschönhausen's industrial area that surrounded the Richard Heike Factory, producer of meat processing machinery.

Initially this restricted area was, after the "military city" in Berlin-Karlshorst, the second largest facility of its kind in the former capital of the German Reich. In the six years it was administered by the Soviets it became a center of terror in the Soviet zone of occupation (SBZ) and again later in the former GDR. It was the site of several remand and prison administration facilities, including:

- the Soviet Special Camp No. 3;
- the Special Camp Administration Department of the Soviet People's Commissariat of Internal Affairs (NKVD), later the Ministry of Internal Affairs (MWD);
- the Central Interrogation and Detention Prison and Central Interrogation Department of the Soviet Ministry of State Security (MGB) in Germany;
- a remand and forced labour camp of the Berlin Operative Department, which initially was under the control of the NKVD and later under the MGB.

The Stalinist denazification and security measures carried out by these facilities caused unspeakable despair for both the victims and their families in Germany. Prior to 1951, approximately 25,000 to 26,000 men and women passed through the remand facilities of this misappropriated industrial area.

Under the direction of the East German Ministry of State Security (MfS) the restricted area served similar functions until the dissolution of the GDR: The Soviet underground prison served as the central remand prison for the MfS and was extensively enlarged with a new addition. A labour camp was located next to this, the so-called Labour Camp X. In addition, the most important units for political persecution were located on this site, including Department XIV (remand and enforcement of sentences) and the Main Investigation Department IX (criminal prosecution). From 1951 to 1989, another 20,000 to 22,000 people passed through the remand center in Berlin-Hohenschönhausen.

The State Security also set up additional department branches in the well-guarded restricted area: Located in the "administrative bureau at Freienwalder Strasse," as this area in Hohenschönhausen was referred to internally, was also Department XII (information/processing/statistics), which had an overview of all the people processed by the MfS and which safeguarded access to the files, which, in the end, measured 180 kilometers. Technical and maintenance departments, as well as the Department of Behind the Lines Services (VRD), were also located here. The large building complex of the Operative Technical Sector (OTS), which developed the surveillance systems, as well as the Armaments Department/ Chemical Services Department (BCD), was also located here. Without the support of these departments the systematic oppression of political opposition in the GDR would never have been possible.

The restricted area in Hohenschönhausen was the second largest administrative center of the State Security Service. In no other part of the Federal Republic of Germany (FRG) is there a comparable collection of architectural bequests of communistic persecution.

This publication provides interested individuals and those visiting the Berlin-Hohenschönhausen Memorial with a comprehensive overview of the GDR Ministry of State Security's formerly restricted area for the first time. It provides detailed information on the history of the various buildings and an overview of the individual secret service departments in the restricted area. A map has been included in the book (pgs. 6/7) to help readers better understand the physical site so that they can explore it on foot without a guide.

The map depicts all buildings and facilities that still existed in 1989/90 and that are still accessible today. In order to avoid confusion, the map is based solely on the existing and designated addresses and building numbers. The large gaps that still exist in research of the restricted area are reflected in the lack of various areas of information.

This historical description of the site is the result of a cooperative project between the Berlin-Hohenschönhausen Memorial and "Der Hain," an employment, qualification and structure development company.

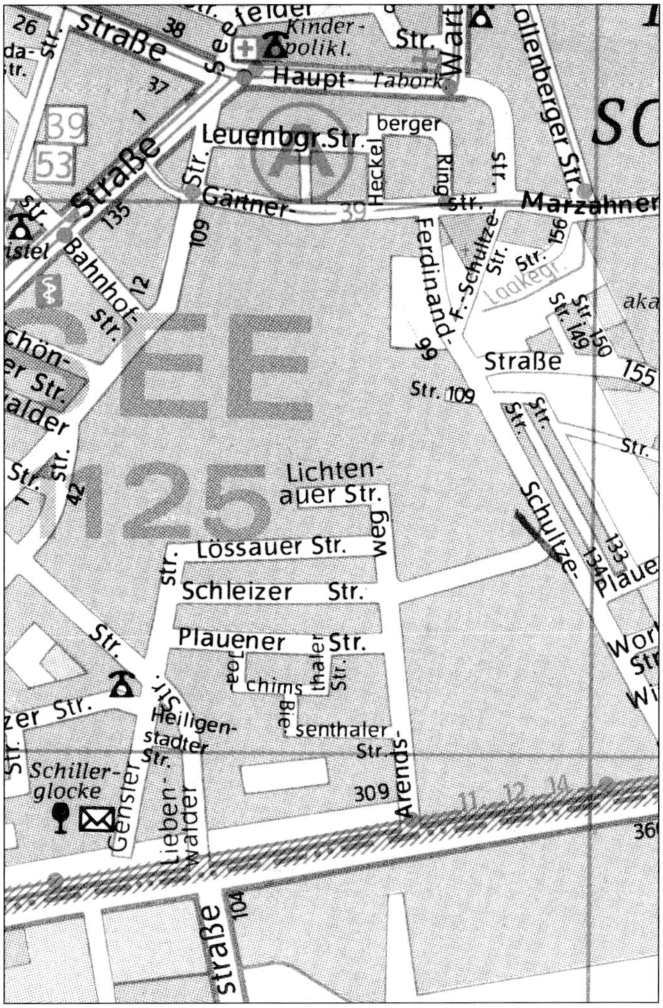

GDR map of Berlin with the restricted area omitted: The streets are simply cut-off (1984)

The introduction describing the history, responsibilities and structures of the Ministry of State Security was written by Dr. Hubertus Knabe. The other contributions were provided by Peter Erler and edited by Hubertus Knabe. Special thanks go to the government-funded organization devoted to the examination and reappraisal of the Communist dictatorship in East Germany (Stiftung zur Aufarbeitung der SED-Diktatur) and the employment office of Berlin-Mitte, which made the research and this publication possible with their financial support.

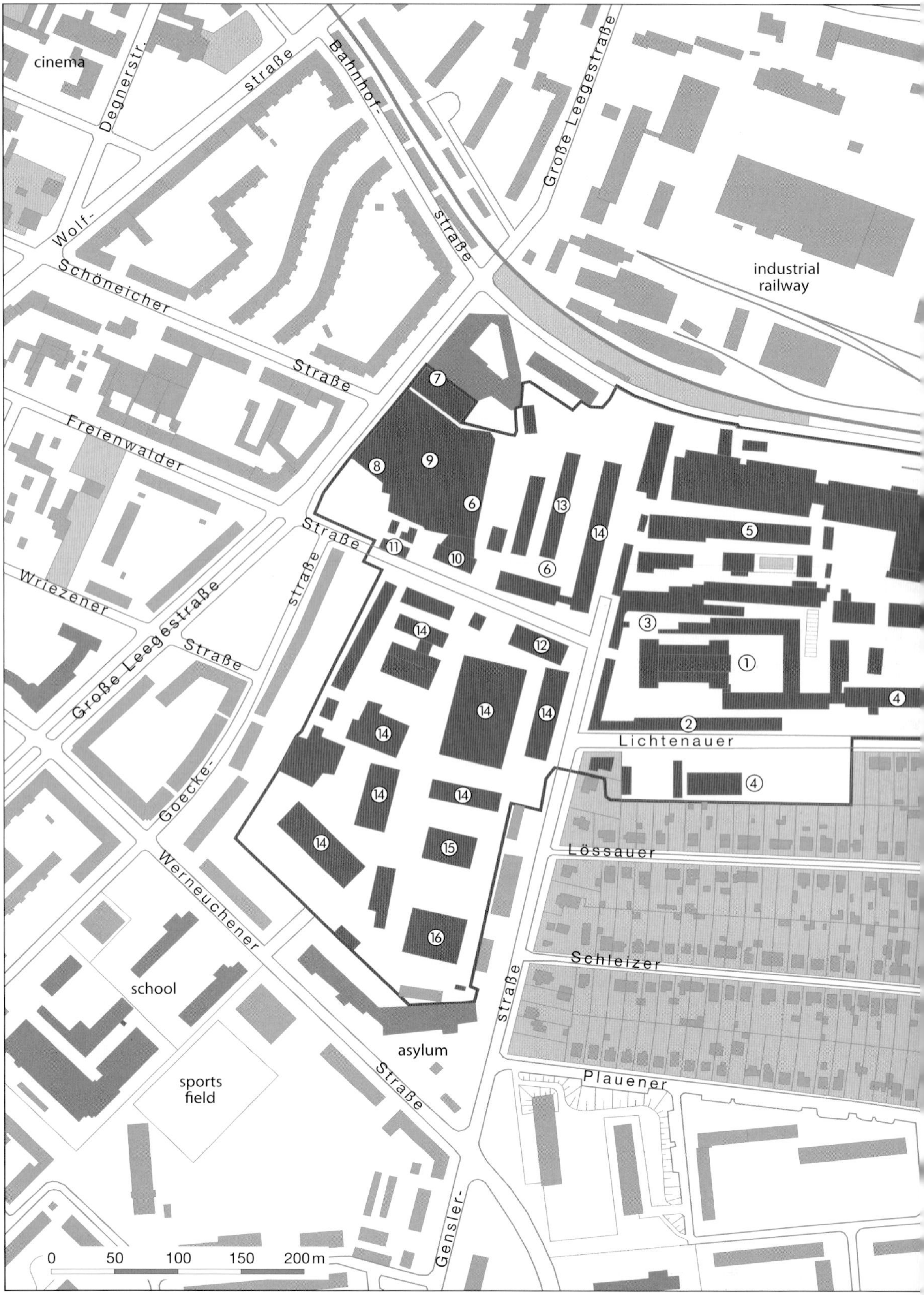
cinema
Degnerstr.
straße
Bahnhof-
straße
Große Leegestraße
industrial railway
Wolf-
Schöneicher
Straße
Freienwalder
Straße
Wriezener
straße
Große Leegestraße
Straße
Goecke-
Werneuchener
Straße
Lichtenauer
Lössauer
Schleizer
Plauener
straße
Gensler-
school
sports field
asylum
① ② ③ ④ ⑤ ⑥ ⑦ ⑧ ⑨ ⑩ ⑪ ⑫ ⑬ ⑭ ⑮ ⑯
0 50 100 150 200 m

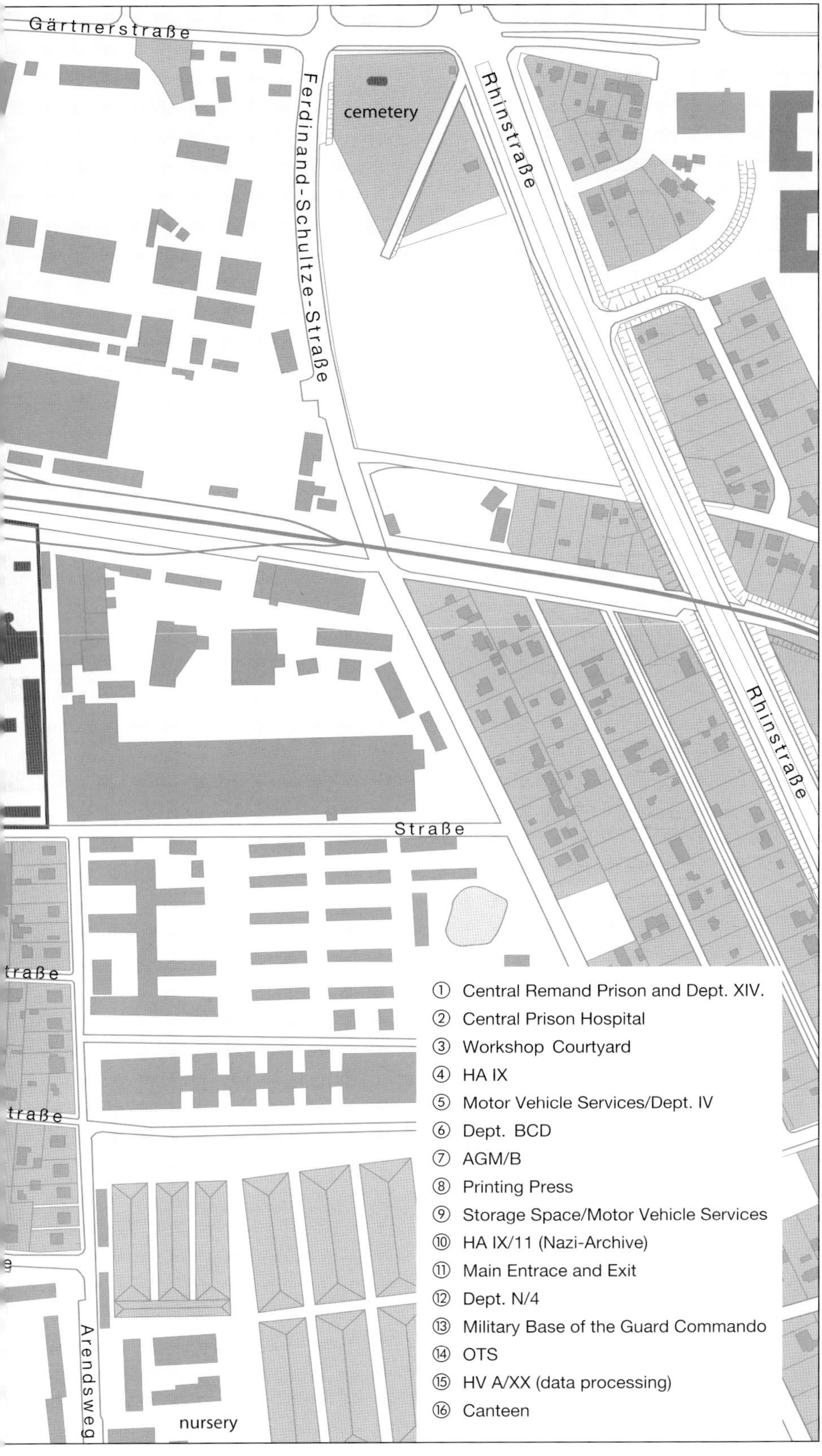

Former restricted area (1990)

The Ministry of State Security

Early History and Growth

Seen formally, the history of the State Security Service (Stasi) began on February 8, 1950, when the parliament of the newly founded German Democratic Republic (GDR) passed a law allowing the creation of the Ministry of State Security (MfS).

Law gazette of the German Democratic Republic (1950)

GESETZBLATT
der
Deutschen Demokratischen Republik

1950	Berlin, den 21. Februar 1950	Nr. 15

Tag	Inhalt	Seite
8. 2. 50	Gesetz über die Bildung eines Ministeriums für Staatssicherheit	95
8. 2. 50	Gesetz über die Teilnahme der Jugend am Aufbau der Deutschen Demokratischen Republik und die Förderung der Jugend in Schule und Beruf, bei Sport und Erholung	95
16. 2. 50	Verordnung über die Neuorganisation des statistischen Dienstes	99
16. 2. 50	Anordnung über die Bildung eines Wissenschaftlich-Technischen Rates zur Überprüfung von Investitionsvorhaben	101
3. 2. 50	Siebente Durchführungsbestimmung zur Anordnung über die Verteilung von industriellen und gewerblichen Waren	101

Gesetz über die Bildung eines Ministeriums für Staatssicherheit.
Vom 8. Februar 1950

§ 1

Die bisher dem Ministerium des Innern unterstellte Hauptverwaltung zum Schutze der Volkswirtschaft wird zu einem selbständigen Ministerium für Staatssicherheit umgebildet. Das Gesetz vom 7. Oktober 1949 über die Provisorische Regierung der Deutschen Demokratischen Republik (GBl. S. 2) wird entsprechend geändert.

§ 2

Dieses Gesetz tritt mit seiner Verkündung in Kraft.
Berlin, den 8. Februar 1950

Das vorstehende, vom Präsidenten der Provisorischen Volkskammer unter dem 10. Februar 1950 ausgefertigte Gesetz wird hiermit verkündet.
Berlin, den 18. Februar 1950

Der Präsident
der Deutschen Demokratischen Republik
W. Pieck

Gesetz
über die Teilnahme der Jugend am Aufbau der Deutschen Demokratischen Republik und die Förderung der Jugend in Schule und Beruf, bei Sport und Erholung.
Vom 8. Februar 1950

Eine gebildete, körperlich gesunde, kräftige, in ihren Auffassungen und ihrem Streben fortschrittliche Jugend sichert ein einheitliches, demokratisches und friedliebendes Deutschland. Die Verfassung der Deutschen Demokratischen Republik hat die grundsätzlichen Voraussetzungen für eine demokratische Erziehung und Entwicklung der deutschen Jugend geschaffen. Nach den in ihr verankerten Grundsätzen ist der Schutz der gesamten Jugend vor Ausbeutung vorgesehen; die geistige, berufliche und körperliche Entwicklung der Jugend und ihre Teilnahme am staatlichen und gesellschaftlichen Leben gewährleistet; die Erziehung der Jugend im Geiste des Friedens, der Freundschaft zwischen den Völkern, wahrer Demokratie und eines echten Humanismus als aktive und bewußte Bürger der neuen demokratischen Gesellschaft festgelegt.

Der deutsche Imperialismus hat die deutsche Jugend mißbraucht. Er hat im Interesse der deutschen Monopolherren und der Junker die gesamte Erziehung der Jugend der Vorbereitung und Führung von Raubkriegen untergeordnet.

In reality, however, the early history of the East German secret police begins much earlier. Its origins go as far back as 1917 in Russia when the Bolsheviks, who came into power through a coup, created their own police apparatus that specifically targeted dissidents. Thousands of people fell victim to the so-called All-Russian Extraordinary Commission for Combating Counter-Revolution and Sabotage, or Cheka for short. The organization, founded by Feliks E. Dzierzynski, was not only a precursor of the Ministry of State Security but its model as well.

Under the general secretary of the Soviet party, Joseph Stalin, terror became the most important characteristic of the communist dictator's secret police. Soon it directed its attention not only against real or alleged opponents of Soviet power, but also against millions of uninvolved parties and even genuine supporters and functionaries. During the "Great Purge" in 1937 and 1938 alone, 1.3 million people were either killed or sentenced to years of detainment in the Gulag.

Following the Second World War the apparatus of the Soviet secret police arrived in the countries of Central and Eastern Europe with the Red Army. It was this group that enforced the restructuring of these countries into communist dictatorships according to the Moscow model. In the Soviet zone of occupation (SBZ) the People's Commissariat and the Ministries of Internal and State Security (the NKVD / NKGB and the MWD / MGB) introduced the operative departments and groups that carried out tens of thousands of arrests in the first years after the war. Not only did they seize nearly all the larger prisons, but countless other structures as well, in the basements of which the arrested individuals were brutally interrogated. During this period more than 150,000 Germans were put into one of ten "special camps" in the SBZ that included the former concentration camps of Buchenwald and Sachsenhausen. Nearly a third of the camp inmates died in detention. Hundreds of thousands of civilians, primarily from the German eastern territories, were deported to the Soviet Union for forced labour, roughly half of whom died.

Under the supervision of the Soviet occupying power, the functionaries of the Communist Party of Germany (KPD) also created their own police apparatus within the SBZ. In 1946 the German Administration of the Interior (DVdI) was established, whose vice president was the logistics manager Erich Mielke, murderer of two German police officers and a fighter in the Spanish Civil War. The so-called Commissariats (K) 5 were responsible for political offences within the DVdI, which now made an increasing number of arrests. In 1949 they were removed from the general criminal investigation department and renamed the Main Administration for the Protection of the National Economy – with Mielke as its director. In February 1950 this was transformed into the Ministry of State Security (MfS), which was headed by the former elementary school teacher and old guard communist, Wilhelm Zaisser (1893–1958), and Mielke became its State Secretary.

Responsibilities and Development

Like its counterpart in the Soviet Union, the GDR's State Security Service primarily functioned as an internally directed secret police. Since the Communists who formed the Socialist Unity Party of Germany (SED) in 1946 had not come into power by means of democratic elections, they felt themselves threatened by countless enemies, causing them to quickly build up their security apparatus accordingly. With over 12,000 employees, the MfS workforce had increased tenfold by 1953. With this it already exceeded that of the prewar Gestapo, which – for the entire German Reich – employed approximately 7,000 workers. Between 1950 and 1952 alone, the MfS recruited about 30,000 informers (IM) in the GDR.

The activities of the State Security Service were directed against all forms of political resistance. Christian democrats, liberal democrats and social democrats were persecuted just as readily as were critical student groups or communists who had become disloyal to the cause. The MfS also combated such organizations as the Task Force Against Inhumanity (KgU), the Investigation Committee of Liberal Lawyers (UfJ) and the East German offices of the CDU, SPD and FDP, which increasingly organized resistance against the SED dictatorship in the West for security reasons. Then, in 1952, the party leader Walter Ulbricht announced the "building up of socialism" and an "intensification of the class struggle." Hundreds of farmers and small businessmen were arrested and their property confiscated. In ad-

Ministry of State Security "sword and shield of the party" emblem

Soviet tank during the popular uprising of June 17, 1953 (Friedrichstrasse in East Berlin)

dition, thousands of workers were arrested because of alleged business offenses. In the course of forced prosecutions, instigated by Moscow, even high-ranking politicians such as the GDR's Secretary of State, Georg Dertinger (CDU), and the long-time member of the SED Politburo, Paul Merker, were arrested. Although the jails were emptied by several mass releases, approximately 67,000 people were still in prison in 1953.

Despite – or perhaps because of – these reprisals, on June 17, 1953, three months after Stalin's death, a sudden uprising in the GDR took place. Hundreds of thousands of people took to the streets and seized town halls, party headquarters and prisons. In many places the local offices of the State Security Service were stormed. Only through the intervention of the Red Army could the uprising be suppressed. At least 13,000 people were arrested and over 1,600 were sentenced to what were often several years of imprisonment. Ulbricht decided to make the State Security Minister, Zaisser – one of his adversaries within the party – responsible for the outbreak of rioting and had him stripped of all duties in July 1953.

REGIERUNG

DER DEUTSCHEN DEMOKRATISCHEN REPUBLIK

DER MINISTERPRÄSIDENT

Ministerium für Staatssicherheit
Genossen Erich M i e l k e

B e r l i n

Nachdem ich der Bitte des Ministers für Staatssicherheit, Genossen Ernst Wollweber, ihn aus Gesundheitsrücksichten von seiner Funktion zu entbinden, entsprochen habe, berufe ich Sie mit Wirkung vom 1. November 1957 zum

Minister
für Staatssicherheit.

Berlin, den 1. November 1957

Letter of appointment for Erich Mielke, issued by the then GDR Minister President, Otto Grotewohl (1957)

The former seaman and communist sabotage specialist, Ernst Wollweber (1898–1967), became the new head of the State Security Service. Initially he only had the status of a state minister when the secret police was integrated into the Interior Ministry, according to the Soviet model. The first assignment the SED gave Wollweber was to search for the West German "backers," who, allegedly, had instigated the uprising of June 17th. It was, above all, because of this event that the State Security developed and intensified its efforts in the West. The until then independent intelligence service directed by the journalist Markus Wolf was incorporated into the secret police and remained part of it until it was dissolved. Several hundred opponents of the regime and defectors – including 120 former MfS employees who had escaped to the West – were kidnapped one by one in the west, brought to the GDR and sentenced to long prison terms. Although the GDR experienced a short thaw following the 20th Party Conference in the Soviet Union in the summer of 1956, by the end of the year – after Soviet troops had crushed the Hungarian uprising – the policy was intensified anew. A series of prominent reform communists, including the philosopher Wolfgang Harich and the publisher Walter Janka, were arrested and imprisoned in the main Stasi remand prison in Berlin-Hohenschönhausen. A year later Wollweber was also dismissed because he did not assume an unconditionally subordinate role to Ulbricht.

In November 1957 Erich Mielke became the head of the State Security Service and was to become the man who would influence the Stasi like no other. He once again carried the title of minister. Shortly after he assumed power, the Soviet "advisors," who, until then, had more or less run the GDR's secret police, were reduced to just several liaison officers. The tremendous inflation of the MfS apparatus began parallel to this. At

Berlin sector crossing at Chausseestrasse shortly after the Wall was built (December 1961)

the end of Mielke's term in office, which lasted more than thirty years, the MfS, with its 91,000 full-time employees, had reached the strength of an army. Statistically speaking this meant that there was one MfS employee per 180 GDR citizens, by which not only Poland (1 : 1574), but also the Soviet Union (1 : 595), was left far behind – not to mention the former FRG, where there was one secret service employee per 4,000 citizens. In addition to this, the MfS also employed approximately 180,000 IMs, who, as secret informers, more or less kept the entire GDR under surveillance. Its budget increased almost annually by more than one hundred million marks and had finally reached more than four billion. These figures express the SED's deep distrust of its own people and a virtually paranoid approach to security that had the goal of identifying early on as many possible dangers to SED domination as possible and eliminating them preclusively.

Until the construction of the Berlin Wall in 1961 the MfS's primary task was to combat the mass tide of refugees from East to West. Because open political protest was not only risky but apparently also pointless, the population's discontentment led to a kind of "referendum with the feet." Each year the GDR lost what in effect was a large city – 2.7 million people by the time the sector borders were closed in Berlin on August 13, 1961. Although the State Security Service maintained that the "enemy" efforts in the GDR were, without exception, inspired by the West, even after the borders in the Berlin sector were sealed off there was no dismantling of the apparatus. On the contrary: the 1960s and 70s saw its fastest period of expansion.

In addition to the classic function of suppression, during this period the State Security Service assumed a series of new activities, which now included both the control of passports and the surveillance of the gradual reintroduction of German-German tourist traffic. The MfS also became more involved in state-owned businesses, establishing its presence there in the form of so-called security administrators and numerous IMs. It also assumed the protection and maintenance of the SED Politburo in Wandlitz. In this context the Commercial Coordination Imperium (KoKo), directed by Alexander Schalck-Golodkowski – an MfS officer in special deployment (OibE) – played an important role in creating a network of businesses that earned millions of marks in foreign currency through illegal business dealings.

The MfS also intensified its activities outside the GDR: Beginning in the mid 1960 s over 3,500 lone fighters were trained to perform acts of sabotage in the West. Following the international recognition of the GDR (1972), the MfS was assigned the task of keeping the newly accredited western diplomats and journalists under surveillance. Shortly after this, a department of "terror resistance" was created, which also trained terrorists of the Red Army Fraction (RAF), to whom the MfS also provided a safe house. The MfS was even active in the Third World.

Although there was almost no public political resistance in the GDR during this period, the State Security Service continued

Warden making his rounds (MfS teaching material, early 1960 s)

to regard the detention and destruction of the "enemy's" aspirations as its duty. In the context of the suppression of the "Prague Spring" by Soviet troops, in 1968 the MfS conducted 500 investigations against GDR citizens who had expressed their sympathy for the socialist reform course in Czechoslovakia. The protests against the expatriation of the songwriter Wolf Biermann in 1976 led to a wave of arrests. Many of the prominent artists who had participated in protests gradually grew disgusted and left the country.

The emphasis on political resignation and intensified surveillance led to a decline in imprisonments during the 1970s. Whereas an average of 3,200 judicial inquiries were conducted every year in the 1950s, this number was reduced by the 1970s to nearly half that. Only in the 1980s did it increase again to 2,500 because of the increasing number of disclosed escape attempts and the growing number of persistent emigration applicants. In 1985 there were 50,000 GDR citizens waiting to emigrate to the West, with the number increasing to 125,000 in 1989, although the SED had already granted about 250,000 such requests – an explosive charge that contributed considerably to the collapse of the GDR. A new increase in the number of arrests also brought additional foreign currency into the country, since the FRG had been paying cash to buy the freedom of each political prisoner since the early 1960s: converted into today's currency that would be approximately 1.75 billion euros for about 34,000 prisoners.

The easing of tension between the East and West that was expressed in these and other dealings did not lead to a dismantling of the MfS apparatus, not even in the later years of the GDR's existence. On the contrary: The State Security Service saw new dangers for the SED system in the stronger German-German contacts and intensified its surveillance activities. With consider-

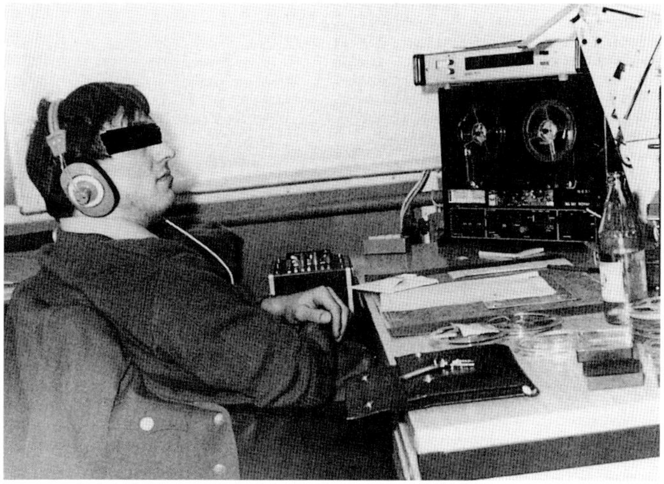

Staff of Main Division III (radio intelligence / radio defense) listening to a tape-recorded telephone conversation

ation to international reactions, the MfS shifted surveillance of the country's population even more into the forefront in order to avoid shootings on the border and spectacular arrests. In addition to the extensive network of secret informers and other similar measures, the systematic monitoring of written correspondence and telephone communication served this end. Using equipment they developed, the MfS opened around 90,000 letters a day and listened in on 20,000 telephones in East Berlin alone. In addition to this, thousands of citizens were monitored in so-called operative procedures (OV) or operative identity checks (OPK) and were subjected to "subversive measures." Thus, the MfS was able to process nearly 5,000 OVs and complete about 8,000 OPKs in the late 1980s.

A kind of state of emergency usually prevailed at major events, such as the annual demonstrations on May 1st, at which hosts of security forces were deployed. When the then West German Chancellor Helmut Schmidt visited the GDR in December 1981, a security force of more than 33,000 ensured that nothing unplanned happened, for the spontaneous calls of "Willy! Willy!" during Willy Brandt's visit to Erfurt in 1970 were still an unpleasant memory for the SED leaders. The MfS also took substantial precautions for potentially explosive situations, during which approximately 11,000 citizens who were classified as "hostile" would be put in isolation camps.

Structures and Operational Methods

Although it may appear so to many, the MfS was in no way a state within the state that could do as it wished. It was, rather, given its orders by the SED, which viewed the State Security Service as its "sword and shield." The long-term duties were – like everything in the GDR – recorded in plans that the SED's Central Committee (ZK) implemented and that created the framework for Erich Mielke's central plan. The MfS was guided politically by the ZK's Department of Security and from an independent SED organization in the ministry. In practice, of course, it was primarily the respective SED head who determined the outlines of the work and who gave instructions regarding individual questions. There existed a similar dependent relationship with the party in the districts and regions of the GDR, since not only did the local SED chairman have the greatest political authority, but he was also the head of the so-called operational command. The Politburo made official decisions regarding arrests and death sentences during the 1950s, and, as of the early 1970s, Honecker and Mielke discussed prevailing security issues in private after meetings.

The MfS, as the party's most important security instrument, possessed a power structure that is only possible in totalitarian states. It combined not only the national and international intelligence service, which were strictly separated from one another in the FRG, but also exercised power over the police and the public prosecution depart-

Erich Mielke, Erich Honecker and Walter Ulbricht (from the left, late 1960s)

ment. In this way it could simultaneously listen in on telephone conversations, intercept letters, deploy secret informers, make arrests, carry out investigations, lock suspected persons up in MfS interrogation prisons and then bring their trials to indictments. By means of its closely linked information network and its access to virtually all government institutions – from schools to doctors to the so-called state-owned businesses, the MfS exercised almost total control over the citizens of the GDR. In fact, as a rule, the centrally directed GDR judiciary executed what the MfS instructed it to and even the execution of sentences was secretly monitored and directed by the MfS with the help of IMs and OibEs. There was as little parliamentary control of the State Security Service as there was the possibility of questioning its methods in an administrative court.

Despite his awkward appearance, Erich Mielke was considered an undisputed authority in the MfS. Not only was he the highest-ranking commander of the militarily structured apparatus, but he also forced those around him to act uncritically and cajolery. On his side were four representatives including the espionage boss, Markus Wolf, who, like Mielke, also headed several departments.

The ministry was composed of more than sixty departments. The Main Investigation Department I, for example, was responsible for monitoring the GDR's military, while the Main Investigation Department II was responsible for "counterespionage," which, above all, most certainly consisted of the precautionary investigation of thousands of uninvolved citizens. The Main Investigation Department III monitored the airwaves, with activities that included listening in on car and international telephone calls conducted in the FRG, including those of the German Chancellor. The Main Investigation Department VI checked passports on the GDR's borders, while the Main Investigation Department VII had the task of monitoring the police and the Interior Ministry. The Main Investigation Department VIII undertook observations and arrests, and the Main Department IX the MfS's preliminary investigations. Furthermore, the most important departments included Departments XIV (interrogation and detention), the Main Departments XVIII (national economy), XIX (post and traffic), XXII (terrorism defense) and XX (state administration, church, art, culture, opposition), all of which, like no other departments, were responsible for the monitoring and persecution of citizens critical of the SED. However, supporting departments, such as Department 26 (monitoring of telephones) and M (monitoring of post), or the Operative Technical Sector (OTS), which built the monitoring devices and carried out criminal investigations, were also very important. Disregarding the Guard Regiment (WR) with more than 11,000 soldiers, the Main Administration A (HV A), which spied on the West, had, with its final headcount of 3,819, more employees than any other department.

The reason for these developments was that the SED and the MfS, already for ideological reasons, had made the FRG the "class enemy," who was first and foremost responsible for each and every homegrown problem. Accordingly, the activities in and towards the "operations area," as the West was called, were considered one of the MfS's main responsibilities. For Mielke it was, therefore, a question of "finding out and using everything that helped the party's politics against the FRG and West Berlin, anything that would shed light on what worked against these politics and that was directed against the GDR Republic." In addition to all the wire tapping devices on the borders and in the diplomatic services in Bonn, a network of 20,000 to 30,000 West German citizens who had been recruited as IMs over four decades also served Mielke's cause. These informers could be found in all important areas of social life, gathering information from business, politics, the military, secret service, and other "enemy areas." Between 1969 and 1987 alone, over 180,000 incoming reports were registered, half of which were forwarded to the Soviet secret service. With the help of agents of influence and so-called "active measures," the MfS tried to affect the political developments in the FRG, above all by supporting protest movements, with IMs in political spheres and through the staging of campaigns against undesirable politicians. In this way the State Security Service saved the former German Chancellor Willy Brandt from losing his position in 1972 by getting two members of the Union Party in the German Parliament to vote against the candidates of their own party in a no-confidence vote. On the other hand, CDU politicians, such as the former Federal President, Heinrich Lübke, and the former President of the Bundestag, Eugen Gerstenmaier, stepped down after the MfS conducted year-long campaigns against them, accusing them of involvement with the Nazis.

It was not only in Berlin that the MfS was equipped with a highly sophisticated apparatus, the headquarters of which were located in an enormous building complex around the Normannenstrasse. Its organizational network, in fact, stretched deep into the districts and regions of the GDR, which had their own MfS bureaus. In each of the fifteen districts – including Berlin – there was a MfS district administration (BV), which had similar departments to those in the headquarters, as well as its own interrogation and remand prisons. The main responsibility for the "security in the territories," however, rested with the 218 MfS regional offices (KD) with their approximately 11,000 employees, who alone controlled more than half of all IMs. In these individual operations, there were also the so-

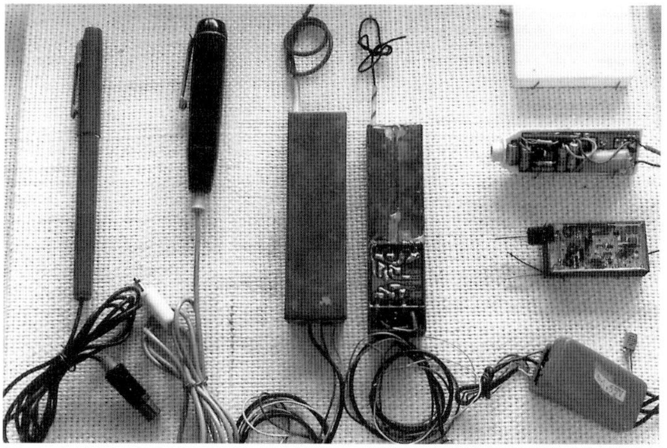

Ministry of State Security wire-tapping equipment

The Ministry of State Security headquarters on Normannenstrasse in Berlin-Lichtenberg (1985)

called administrative bureaus, for example at Carl-Zeiss-Jena or the chemical combine Bitterfeld. The local and regional branches of the MfS were answerable to the respective director on site but were directly connected to headquarters via the so-called principle of lines. In this way the most important departments in Berlin could fall back on employees in the districts and counties at any time.

As Mielke never tired of stressing, the informers formed the "main weapon" of the MfS. Despite growing technological possibilities, the secret informers were still considered to be the most important and reliable method of monitoring the activities of others. Such informers did not report spontaneously or coincidentally but were recruited and deployed on the basis of a more or less academic analysis. For decades experts at the MfS Law School in Potsdam occupied their time with the question of how people could be brought to denounce others and dozens of MfS employees dedicated their master's and doctoral theses to the topic.

Preparation and deployment of IMs were regulated according to extensive guidelines. Before being recruited the candidates in question would be closely examined as a rule, in order to find out just how they would react to a recruitment proposal. Finally the responsible MfS officer would write a submittal in which he would outline the course of events for the planned recruitment that had to be signed by his superior. Only after this procedure was completed would the candidate be approached, and ideally, the contact would result in his signing a declaration of commitment. In difficult cases – for instance with priests or West Germans – the MfS made do with a gradual involvement because it was not the signature that was crucial, but rather the willingness to secretly cooperate. Only around one percent of GDR citizens, however, were willing to cooperate with the MfS and a third of all planned recruitments failed, something that is often forgotten in discussions about Stasi involvement in the East.

Although the Stasi had instructions not to recruit informers from the ranks of the SED when possible, ultimately over thirty percent were, in fact, party members.

The MfS divided its IMs into various categories. An IM for the "protection against conspiracy" (IMK), as it was officially called, was, for instance, an East German who allowed the MfS to use his apartment or telephone for secret meetings. There were also IMs who intentionally spied on their fellow citizens in the "immediate handling of people who were under suspicion for enemy activities" (IMB) and who carried out assignments for their superiors. Between these two poles there was a series of other categories, the largest of which was the group of IMs in charge of the "political-operative penetration and safeguarding of the responsible departments" (IMS). Such an IM was a kind of semi-official informant in an apartment building, a school, a business, etc., who conspiratorially cooperated with the MfS.

The IMs were, above all, and depending on their area of activity, responsible for reporting on their personal or work environment. It was particularly the IMBs, who comprised two percent of all IMs, who were assigned to "enemy" individuals in order to sound them out and influence or combat them. The superior officers met the IMs every four to six weeks as a rule, usually in a safe flat or sometimes only briefly in an automobile. At such meetings the officers received written or verbal reports and gave new assignments. In these situations the MfS stressed the IM's honesty, which was checked at regular intervals. As a rule the work was rewarded with little more than small gifts or the occasional medal. All this was precisely recorded in a dossier, which included a personal report and, if applicable, a financial one.

From this network of informers and the monitoring of letters and telephone conversations, the MfS always had an abundance of evidence that was promptly forwarded to the appropriate department. In addition to this it also conducted so-called security checks, which, above all, concerned people with leadership responsibilities. According to Erich Mielke, the main question behind all these activities was: "Who is who?" The MfS would learn as much as possible about what each citizen thought and if he was dependable from a political point of view.

Once a person attracted suspicion, the State Security Service would often set up a kind of initial file, which would be converted into an operative personal check (OPK) or an operative process (OV) should the suspicions be substantiated. This meant that an MfS officer investigated the said individual systematically, according to a written plan. As a rule, confidants in the workplaces or housing estates were questioned, written correspondence and telephone calls were monitored and various IMs were given specific orders for this purpose. Whereas precautionary surveillance was the dominant aim of the OPK – which could occasionally lead to the recruiting of someone – the OV already assumed that the person had committed a concrete offence. Without the knowledge of the affected person and using secret service methods, the MfS conducted investigations against the said person relat-

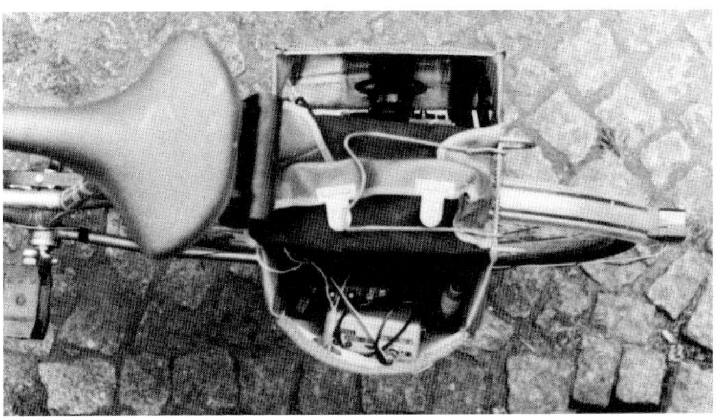

MfS surveillance camera, disguised as a bike saddle bag

ing to accusations of, for instance, treason, planning to cross the border or subversive agitation.

When a person was arrested, the State Security Service often already knew all about the offence of which he was accused. The detainee was sent to one of seventeen MfS remand centers, where a formal preliminary investigation was begun. In accordance with Mielke's guidelines to take precautions against undesired behavior, the MfS often reacted to an offence while it was still in its planning stage, for which GDR criminal law provided ample opportunities. The so-called investigation leader tried to get the offender – who was subjected to solitary confinement and degrading chicaneries – to make a confession during what could be weeks or months of interrogation in order to complete and "officialize" the MfS's findings, meaning to make them applicable in court. In this period the detainee typically had no contact with either family members or a lawyer so that the interrogator was his only human contact, other than with security personnel. Finally, the MfS drew up a final report, which served as the basis for the indictment. The statements made by the detainee during the interrogation served as evidence in court, even if he later revoked them. The sentence corresponded almost exactly with the MfS's allegations. The number of people arrested in the GDR for political reasons is estimated at 200,000 to 250,000.

In order to improve its international reputation, the SED increasingly tried to avoid arresting critics during the 1970s and 1980s. Prominent opponents, such as Ulrike Poppe, Freya Klier and Bärbel Bohley, were released just days after participating in protests. Often less obvious methods of persecution were used, especially if someone had contacts in the West. Rather than arresting the person in question, he would be – as provided for in the OV guideline 1/76 – "shattered, paralyzed, confused and isolated," without the MfS's appearing as the instigator. The list of these methods stretches from the systematic discrediting of one's

Arrest by the MfS

I had to get dressed quickly, my every step watched by a Stasi man. I quickly stuck some money in my pocket and then all hell broke loose. Several Ladas were parked outside the front door. One drove off, leading, another followed; I sat on the seat, handcuffed, wearing metal glasses, and I wasn't supposed to know where we were going.
The drive ended after we had passed through several heavy metal gates, which you could tell from all the stopping and the short orders being given and then, at some point, I had to get out. The glasses were taken off and I saw a small garage with an exit. Then I was ordered inside and had to undress, put everything on a table, then the things were taken away. After that I was examined, they looked in all my orifices. Then I got prisoner's clothes. These consisted of a jogging outfit and slippers, nothing else, with a pair of gym shorts and top as underwear. Then I was led through lots of corridors and locked into a cell.

For political reasons, Klaus Freymuth was arrested in July 1984 for allegedly violating customs laws and tax evasion and was detained until March 1985 in Berlin-Hohenschönhausen.
Source: Gilbert Furian: Mehl aus Mielkes Mühlen. Schicksale politisch Verurteilter. Berichte, Briefe, Dokumente. Berlin, 1991, pgs. 73–74.

Corridor of the new prison building (photo from November 1990)

public reputation to the intentional organization of professional failures to the artificial creation of distrust and mutual suspicions.

For this the MfS depended, above all, on its IMs, who intentionally spread rumors, stirred up conflict or unnerved the affected person, who was put under additional pressure and influenced by so-called partners of the operative cooperation (POZW) – superiors, teachers, police, doctors, etc. Relationships with family members and friends were intentionally destroyed by using anonymous letters and compromising photographs. The state organized psychological terror to which several thousand people were exposed, often over a period of many years, and whose systematically planned effects were controlled by MfS officers. It was a "quiet form of terror," as the writer Jürgen Fuchs described it, who himself had been a victim of endless subversive actions that once characterized MfS activities.

Decline and Dissolution

While the SED's need for international recognition and its growing economic problems in the GDR had forced the MfS since the beginning 1980s to make more intense considerations of its behavior vis-à-vis the West, in 1986 a surprising second front opened up in the East: the reform politics of the new Soviet party headed by Mikhail Gorbachev, who tried to save the ailing socialist system with "Glasnost" (openness) and "Perestroika" (reconstruction). Although the SED's main ideologist, Kurt Hager, tried to dismiss the problem in 1988 with the comment that "one doesn't re-wallpaper his apartment just because his neighbor does," the GDR, in fact, stood without its political protector for the first time since its establishment. This had serious after-effects for the GDR's stability: demands, which up until then had only been made by the "class enemy," could now be made by critics within the GDR society with reference to the propaganda slogan,

"Learning from the Soviet Union means learning to win!" Doubt about the party's approach came even from within the SED's own ranks, for instance when, in November 1989, it was prohibited from selling the German-language Soviet magazine "Sputnik" in the GDR. The politics of the SED became increasingly entangled in contradictions because, on the one hand, it could not abandon reprisals, and on the other hand, it became more and more dependent on international cooperation. In order to avoid becoming completely isolated, the GDR saw itself forced to agree to allow human rights groups into its country at the follow up Conference on Security and Cooperation in Europe (KSZE) in 1988 in Vienna, something that the State Security Service had vehemently opposed until then. It also became increasingly easy for GDR citizens to travel to the West, with the result that they became increasingly discontent with their own living conditions.

.The security-political dilemma for the SED became blatantly apparent for the first time when the State Security Service searched the rooms of the oppositional Umweltbibliothek (environment library), in order to crush the magazine "Grenzfall," which had been published unofficially for a year. After an infiltrated IM suggested publishing the paper in the rooms of the Zion's Church parish house and had informed the MfS of the date this was to happen, a group of about twenty Stasi officers, together with the chief public prosecutor, appeared on the night of November 24th in the East Berlin parish house in order to catch the initiators in the act of printing the leaflet. Several employees of the Umweltbibliothek were arrested and the printing machines confiscated. The very next day, however, a solidarity campaign – including vigils and intercessions – was instigated and quickly made public through West German television. The SED ordered the State Security Service to let the detainees go after a few days, which represented a clear victory for the relatively small GDR opposition. The situation was repeated in January 1988, when the MfS arrested several political opponents and emigration applicants, who had carried banners in an official memorial demonstration to Rosa Luxemburg and Karl Liebknecht. Although the State Security Service managed to get several leading opponents to leave the GDR this time, a few managed to be granted the right to return, once again making the weakness of the SED obvious. After this, the independent peace, environmental and human rights groups which were protected by the Protestant church became more and more popular – not least with numerous emigration applicants who had high hopes of being able to emigrate quickly to the FRG.

In May 1989 opposition groups protested against the falsification of local election results, which, for the first time, did not reflect an approval rating of 99 percent by eligible voters, as had been the case in the past. That summer countless GDR citizens sought refuge in the West German embassies in Prague and Budapest and demanded, once and for all, to be allowed to emigrate to the

Border guards of the National People's Army in the Potsdamer Platz train station

West. After the Hungarian government pulled down its border with Austria, for all to see, hundreds of GDR citizens finally walked over the grassed border without the State Security Service being able to do a thing about it. The images of the smiling refugees that appeared on West German television refuted not only the insistent success propaganda in the East German media but also made the SED's own helplessness obvious, while those who were left behind felt more and more like they were on a sinking ship. Under these conditions a growing number of people demonstrated each Monday in Leipzig, demanding reform in the GDR and a political dialogue between the people and government. Once again, the State Security Service was unable to stop them effectively. In early October a domestic political crisis culminated when the SED celebrated the GDR's fortieth anniversary while over 70,000 people marched through the inner city of Leipzig. Under these circumstances the Politburo forced Erich Honecker to resign on October 18, 1989 and named Egon Krenz as his successor.

The new SED leadership announced political change and the introduction of reforms. The most important top officials, including Erich Mielke, lost their posts and became scapegoats. In mid-November, amidst the relieving laughter of the delegates, Mielke, who just recently had been so feared, defended himself with the now-famous sentences: "I love, but I love everyone. But I love ..." Three weeks later he was arrested and imprisoned on remand, spending part of the time in the prison hospital in Berlin-Hohenschönhausen.

Wolfgang Schwanitz, a former wholesaler and Mielke's representative until then, became the new head of the State Security Service, which was simultaneously renamed the Agency for National Security (AfNS). Of course this could not pacify the extensive public rage against the Stasi. When it became known that files were being systematically destroyed behind the walls of the Stasi building, citizens occupied district administration buildings for the first time in early December 1989. It was under these conditions that the GDR government decided on December 14 to dissolve the AfNS as well and replace it with a federal agency for internal security and an intelligence service – in vain. Under pressure from the ongoing civil protests, in January 1990 the government saw itself forced to phase out the State Security Service without a substitute by March 31, although the HV A was granted until June 31 to do this. In order to accelerate the Service's dissolution, demonstrators also occupied the Stasi headquarters on Normannenstrasse on January 15, 1990 and, from that point on, a citizen's committee, together with a government representative, watched over the dismissal of the 91,000 full-time employees, as well as the preservation of the files. It soon became clear that the MfS was also embedded in the newly founded opposition parties in leading positions with IMs, including the chairman of the CDU-sympathetic "Demokratischer Aufbruch" (democratic awakening), Wolfgang Schnur, and the top candidate for the Social Democrats, Ibrahim Böhme, both of whom were then forced to resign. A total of more than 125,000 revolvers and 77,000 machine guns were collected from the offices of the MfS – a stockpile of weapons that made the bloodless dissolution of the State Security Service seem a wonder.

Erich Mielke was never held legally accountable for his actions as Minister of the State Security Service – like most other MfS employees. Only in 1993 was he convicted to a six-year prison sentence for the murder of the two policemen on Berlin's Bülowplatz, a crime he had committed at the end of the Weimar Republic. He was paroled just two years later and died on May 21, 2000 in a nursing home.

The Restricted Area

Early History

The Berlin district of Hohenschönhausen is closely connected to the history of the GDR's State Security Service. Originally the area was a small Niederbarnimish village, which was the property of the Prussian Administrative District of Potsdam until 1920. The suburban community's urban development began at the end of the 19th century after the land around the former manor there was divided into lots and sold. Industrial companies settled to the south of the Sandpfuhl and to the east of Berliner Strasse (today the Konrad-Wolf-Strasse) that profited decisively from the construction of the industrial railway Tegel-Friedrichsfelde. The first section – the stretch between Friedrichsfelde and Blankenburg – was opened on December 16, 1907. That same year the Hohenschönhausen goods station, which would later become the detention center, was opened.

In 1910 the businessman Richard Heike purchased a 15,000 square meter piece of land located on the corner of Grosse-Leege-Strasse 95–96 and Freienwalder Strasse 17–19 and had a factory for meat processing machines built there, as well as an administrative building. The "Heike Factory" started production in the spring of 1911 with 250 employees and became one of the largest employers in Hohenschönhausen. The products – machines and equipment for butcher shops and sausage factories, appliances for the production and the sealing of tin cans, as well as systems for slaughterhouses and the lard industry – were in demand both nationally and internationally.

In the following years Richard Heike bought additional pieces of property in the area: Bahnhofstrasse 7–9, Freienwalder

View of the "Heike Factory" from the corner of Grosse-Leege-Strasse / Freienwalder Strasse (1937)

▷ Business signs of some of the companies located within the restricted area until 1945

Strasse 15/16 and Genslerstrasse 66–72. "He leased most of this land, as well as the buildings on it, to other companies. Just like the other companies that had settled around Heike's property, they, too, profited from the siding that forked off from the industrial railway at Grosse-Leege- and Bahnhofstrasse. The area was officially declared an industrial zone in the 1920s at the request of the entrepreneur.

Several new companies had to halt their production because of the world economic crisis at the end of the 1920s, including the Berlin-Aachen mirror producer Röder, Meyer und Co., established in 1912 and located at Freienwalder Strasse 12a, as well as the enamel and sheet metal factory of Ludwig Winterberg in Schöneicher Strasse that had been in business since 1911. Other companies, however, were very successful and became leaders in their fields, as was the case with the company Albrecht Reiser at Genslerstrasse 15, manufacturer of road construction machinery, and the Max Uhlendorf factory at Goeckestrasse 37–38, which made industrial electric furnaces.

The establishment of the National Socialist regime in 1933 was not without consequences for the Hohenschönhausen industrial area. The Jewish businessmen were forced to sell their property and companies, in accordance with racist laws of the time. Those who profited from these coercive measures were, among others, the Berlin button factory Koch & Co., "Bekafa," at Genslerstrasse 15–16 and the Coal Separating Limited Liability Company at Freienwalder Strasse 14–16. In 1940 the owner of the last Jewish business on the site, the Hartwig Kontorowicz Company, was also forced to sell his property. The lot at Grosse-Leege-Strasse 97–98, as well as all the buildings on it, went to the liqueur and brandy manufacturer C. A. F. Kahlbaum AG. With this the Hohenschönhausen industrial area was completely "aryanized."

Military and National Socialist facilities started to settle in the neighborhood. In 1937 the Ministry of Aviation Treasury bought a building at Freienwalder Strasse 12 a. A year later, on October 4, 1938, the Berlin district Nazi head purchased a 10,000 square meter piece of property from the entrepreneur Heike, which had only been used for agricultural purposes until then and would later become the heart of the restricted area.

On the lot on Genslerstrasse, later given the house number 66, the National Socialist People's Welfare Organization (NSV) built a modern canteen for the Winter Welfare Association at the request of the NSDAP. Several auxiliary structures were also erected, such as guardhouses, garages and a laundry house with two three-room personnel apartments. Soon hundreds of people worked in the two story "food factory," which had a basement and could prepare 30,000 meals on a single workday.

The Second World War represented a disastrous break for the Hohenschönhausen industrial area. Although the attacks on Poland, France, the Soviet Union and other countries initially ensured full order books, this made the collapse in 1945 all the worse.

Thanks to armament orders and supplies for the military, the businesses in Hohenschönhausen were often able to increase their profits in the first years of the war and various businesses had to expand their production. The Corporation for Rust Protection at Bahnhofstrasse 7–9 erected a new storage and appliance facility to accommodate an order for the Navy High Command in 1939/40. The company "Erwin Neuendorf. Häute und Felle. Import-Export" (Erwin Neuendorf's Animal hides and Furs Import-Export Company) at Genslerstrasse 69–72 applied to the municipal buildings inspection department for various extension permits after they were appointed "the distribution center for hides and furs for the Military District III" in May 1940 by the Reich's Leather Trade Department.

The war also forced more and more male workers to be drafted to the front. The jobs they left were now primarily taken over by prisoners of war and forced labourers. Around one hundred prisoners from the prisoner of war camp, Stalag III D, who had to make parts for tanks, ammunition and rifle butts, camped out in a reconstructed shed at Genslerstrasse 67. Because of the growing need for personnel, Richard Heike had additional barracks built in November 1942 to house foreign forced labourers.

A second camp was built next door in 1942/43 for the vaccine manufacturer Asid at Genslerstrasse 68. The Polish and so-called "Eastern workers" from the Ukraine and Russia, had to work in the company's serum institute and sheet metal shop.

As of 1942 a field building of the re-education work camp in Wuhlheide was also located on the lot belonging to the Ministry of Aviation Treasury at Freienwalder Strasse 12a. In addition to Jewish prisoners, "Eastern workers," who supposedly did not fulfill their work requirements or had violated codes of discipline, were the primary residents in this prison camp run by the Gestapo. These prisoners, numbering about fifty, had to level a fallow piece of land at Goeckestrasse 40–42. The Wehrmacht then constructed a collecting point for military loot on the site.

In the time that followed additional military structures were erected in the neighborhood of the industrial area. Thus the businessman and pig farmer Wilhelm Steinke transferred the majority of his property at Gärtnerstrasse 19–26 to the Military District Headquarters III in Berlin-Grunewald in December 1942. The next year the Military Administration had a map depot built here that included several barracks.

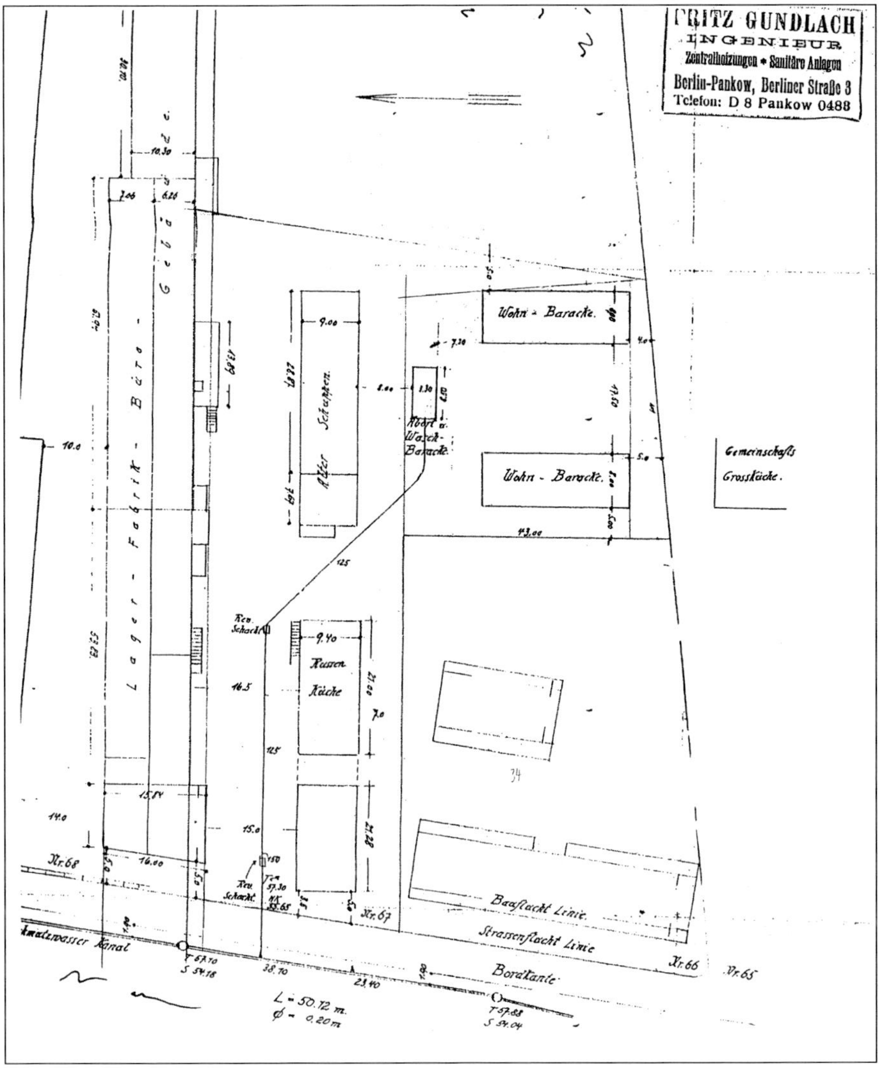

Sewage system map for the forced labourers of the Asid vaccine manufacturer on Genslerstrasse, part of Special Camp No. 3 by June 1945 (1942/43)

Soon destruction from bomb attacks became another consequence of the war. No other city in Europe experienced as many air raids as Berlin did. In Hohenschönhausen the bombers primarily attacked industrial production sites near the industrial railway and its track and train station facilities, as well as military buildings. The company names Asid, Kahlbaum and Heike appeared time and time again in damage reports.

In May 1944 the button factory "Bekafa" was badly hit and considered from this point on to be bombed out. Berlin experienced one of its most serious air raids on March 18, 1945. In Hohenschönhausen firebombs destroyed the Asid research laboratories and damaged a large part of the meat processing machinery factory.

In April 1945 during a heavy bomb attack, residents from Lichtenauer and Lössauer Strasse sought refuge in the enormous basement and storage spaces of the NSV canteen. On April 4, 1945 demolition bombs killed ten Soviet forced labourers in a splinter trench on the Asid property and destroyed two housing barracks at Genslerstrasse 67.

Soviet Era (1945–1951)

On April 22, 1945 the First White Russian Front, a division of the 5th Shock Army, captured the Berlin district of Hohenschönhausen under its commander in chief, Nikolaj E. Bersarin. While the fighting troops pushed forward toward the city center, other troops secured the already captured hinterland. In Hohenschönhausen they occupied German army buildings and other important facilities, such as the industrial train station. The Red Army confiscated supplies stored in the Neuendorf and Asid companies on Genslerstrasse.

In the short period between the collapse of German administration and the establishment of an occupying regime, many things changed ownership in one way or the other. By the end of 1945 not only did the abundantly stored inventory of food disappear from the NSV canteen, but technical appliances, panes of glass and other objects that could be used for building or bartering as well.

During this time, in which bitter battles were still being fought in the inner city, several acts of revenge, at times instigated by forced labourers, occurred. On April 23 the 80-year-old factory owner Richard Heike, his housekeeper Gertrud Häussler and Arthur Minke, a family friend, were shot by Soviet soldiers on the corner of Freienwalder Strasse 14/Genslerstrasse 13. These kinds of liquidations numbered in the thousands in eastern Germany.

The operative group of the Soviet counterespionage unit "SMERSH" ("death to spies") and the Moscow Soviet People's Commissariat of Internal Affairs (NKVD) followed quickly on the heels of the White Russian Front's fighter troops. As early as late April 1945 they conducted numerous arrests in Hohenschönhausen, usually following denunciations. Among those arrested was the junior partner of the meat processing machinery factory and the founder's son of the same name, Richard Heike. The engineer, born in 1903, was sent to the so-called special camp in Mühlberg, from which he was deported to the Soviet Union in February 1947. He died there on July 7, 1949 in a forced labour camp in the Urals. The director of the demolition company at Genslerstrasse 17/18, Moritz Barth, went into NKVD custody after he was accused of reporting Jews to the Gestapo.

Parallel to such arrests, the NKVD established a restricted military area in Hohenschönhausen and also built a camp. In mid May the director of the Special Camp Administration Department under the First White Russian Front, Colonel Michail E. Swiridow, ordered the establishment of Special Camp No. 3. A NKVD unit headed by the camp's future director, Major Smaroda, took possession of the canteen site and the two National Socialist forced labour camps at Genslerstrasse 66–67. Presumably there were several reasons for choosing this site.

The good railway connection made the area attractive since the Hohenschönhausen industrial area was just adjacent to it and the site was also located in a relatively isolated part of Berlin's outskirts and away from any large residential areas. The existing buildings could also be restructured without much effort.

On June 7, 1945 a total of 110 prisoners started erecting the roadblock on Genslerstrasse and carrying out other necessary alteration work. These men had been transferred to Hohenschönhausen from the Soviet Special Camp Landsberg/Warthe

Special Camp No. 3 stamp

expressly for this purpose. At the order of the local Hohenschönhausen commander, German workers were also mobilized for reconstruction work and repairs. The windows in all parts of the buildings had to be replaced following the bombings and the looting at the end of the war. The glasswork and the materials necessary to execute the work consumed four-fifths of the submitted construction costs, a total of 4492.65 marks. The actual occupation of Special Camp No. 3 by prisoners from Berlin and its surroundings began in late June 1945.

The camp's guard detail was probably initially housed in rooms of the Asid Serum Institute. On June 17, 1945 members of these convoy troops got drunk on methyl alcohol with grave consequences: 27 people, including six prisoners, had to be admitted to the military hospital on Küstriner Strasse with serious poisoning symptoms and five members of the Red Army died.

With the construction of the special camp on the lot behind the Hohenschönhausen industrial train station (Gärtnerstrasse 19–26/ Ferdinand-Schulze-Strasse 95–99), this area was also withdrawn from civil use. On this site a farmyard was created on which former Soviet war prisoners kept cows, horses, pigs and sheep for use by the camp personnel. Dead soldiers were also buried here.

Working together with the German administrative facilities, several company owners and personnel tried to free the works in the industrial area from the war rubble during this time. Production was to begin again, adjusted to current needs. The NKVD, however, had other plans. It was probably in the second half of July 1945 that the NKVD's representative in the SBZ, Colonel General Iwan A. Serow, decided to expand the restricted area. The area by Freienwalder/Genslerstrasse was to accommodate a prison labour camp (HAL), as well as the Special Camp Department, which was directly subordinate to it and which had had its headquarters in Fürstenwalde until then. This department was responsible for all Soviet internment camps in Germany. They had already begun working in Hohenschönhausen in early July. The offices and the archive affiliated with the department were housed in the administration building of the former Neuendorf Company at Genslerstrasse 69–72. At the same time the eviction of approximately two hundred owners and tenants from their homes in the housing development in the Lichtenauer and Lössauer Strasse also began.

In the middle of July 1945 General Major Aleksej M. Sidnew, head of the Operative Department in Berlin, part of the NKVD apparatus, ordered the construction of a prison labour camp that was euphemistically referred to as an "industry combine." The "Heike Factory," four other factories near it and the German army's collection depot for military loot were taken over by the Red Army for this purpose. The works were stripped and disassembled, in part by prisoners from Special Camp No. 3, and by March 1946 they had gradually been incorporated into the restricted military area. In June/July 1946 the Asid Company also had to vacate its facilities, which were also taken over by the Special Camp Department. The land and buildings were shielded from the outside world with wire mesh and barbed wire. As they had already done when they established the special camp, for this task, too, the NKVD made use of the stockpiles

"Ivan the Terrible"

The chief officer responsible for the repression apparatus in the Soviet zone of occupation was Colonel General Ivan Alexandrowitsch Serow. Born in 1905, the Russian joined the Communist Party in 1926 and the Red Army two years later. When he was thirty he was sent to the staff college and immediately became one of the most ambitious young cadres in the Communist Party of the Soviet Union (CPSU).

In 1939 he entered the NKVD as Third Deputy Commissar of State Security and shortly thereafter became the People's Commissar of Internal Affairs and a member of the Politburo in the Ukraine. There he made a name for himself, above all, with the brutal integration of the part of Poland that had been annexed by the Soviet Union in 1939 and of the Baltic States. Under his supervision a large number of the national ruling class were murdered or deported to labour camps. Following the German attack on the Soviet Union in 1941, and as Deputy People's Commissar of State Security and then Internal Affairs of the USSR, he organized the deportation to the east of the Volga Germans who were collectively considered to be traitors. In October Stalin appointed him head of the Moscow Defense Zone. In 1943/44 he carried out the deportation of the Caucasian people, as well as of the Kalmyks and the Crimeans. Following the reconquest of the Ukraine, Poland and the Baltic, Serow was in these countries for a second time on duty for the NKVD and organized new deportations. In January 1945 he became NKVD commissioner with the First White Russian Front and, with this appointment, became responsible for "cleansing the hinterland" while advancing on Berlin.

Following Germany's capitulation Serow became master of two Soviet security services in Germany. As acting head of the Soviet Military Administration for Germany (SMAD), for civilian matters and the acting head of the NKVD in the Soviet zone of occupation, he was not just responsible for the two secret services, NKVD and NKGB, but also for all camps and prisons. He was thus sometimes referred to as "Ivan the Terrible" by the Berlin military administration.

In 1947 Serow became First Deputy of Internal Affairs of the USSR while maintaining his functions in Germany. In 1954 he became head of the Committee for State Security (KGB) and fulfilled a leading position in the crushing of the Hungarian Uprising in 1956. In 1958 he became head of the Soviet Union's Main Intelligence Directorate (GRU) and vice chairman of the chief of staff of the Soviet armed forces.

The mass murderer's decline began in the 1960s. Following the escape of a high-ranking GRU employee to the "enemy operation area," Serow was demoted to general major and then demoted to commander's assistant of the military district Turkestan – he retired on September 1, 1965. That same year he was expelled from the CPSU because of a "breach of rule of law during his services in Germany." Serow died in Moscow on July 1, 1990 without having ever been held legally accountable for his deeds.

from the Josef Berthoty wire factory at Genslerstrasse 13, which was now also part of the restricted area.

Following the expansion of the restricted area, the main entrance and the access road were relocated to Freienwalder Strasse. A

Unhinged Windows and Fences

As has just been reported, the [Soviet] soldiers are dismantling the apartments on Lössauer Strasse. Window frames, for example, are being unhinged, the glass is being removed and the empty frames are being thrown onto a pile. Stationary furnaces and stoves are also being removed. It has even been reported that wooden stairs are being dismantled. These objects are apparently being used to develop facilities on Lichtenauer Strasse; because of this many apartments on Lössauer Strasse are regrettably being abandoned to the elements, and will thus become uninhabitable over time. Perhaps relief is possible by negotiating with the district commander. – The Asid Company is located next to the concentration camp and, through the restoration and new construction of a fence, to be included in it. We have approached the commander, who has promised to inhibit [= to impose a stop to] the plan's execution. The Asid Company also feels compelled to transfer its production to the American sector.

Report excerpts from the local district office Hohenschönhausen to the mayor of Weissensee dated October 18 and December 7, 1945.
Source: LAB, Rep. 148/1, No.12 and 19.

barrier and watchtower were situated right behind Goeckestrasse, both manned by military guards. The iron gate, at which there was briefly contact with the outside world in the early weeks of occupation, was already boarded up during the summer of 1945.

In October 1946 Serow ordered the prisoners of Special Camp No. 3 to be transferred to the former concentration camp in Sachsenhausen. He transferred the site at Genslerstrasse 66–67 to the Soviet Ministry of State Security (MGB), which held the remaining barracks for Nazi prisoners of war, and had the Nazi forced labour camps demolished and the central remand prison in Germany set up in the former canteen. The oft provisional structures were demolished. Prisoners occupied the newly created windowless main wing located in the basement of the canteen, the so-called "U-Boot" ("the submarine") for the first time in the spring of 1947.

The establishment of the remand center led to further expansions of the restricted area. The MGB personnel needed living space and parking lots for their official vehicles. Lots and buildings in the western part of Grosse-Leege-Strasse, between Wriezener Strasse and Bahnhofstrasse, were added in 1947/1948.

The MGB occupied the dwellings of about sixty tenants and the garages and industrial area belonging to Ludwig Winterberg on Schöneicher Strasse, as well as a partially fallow lot filled with the ruins of an education authority building at Freienwalder Strasse 6a–8. Soviet soldiers planted vegetables and potatoes on this open space. The restricted area thus had access to another self supply facility next to the farm behind Bahnhofstrasse. As of 1947 the factory grounds of the Richard Thiele Company at Goeckestrasse 39 were also incorporated into the restricted area.

On June 16, 1947 the light rail service through the Hohenschönhausen industrial area was discontinued. A barrier and an iron gate now blocked the dead end tracks – which ran across the restricted area – on both sides. The connection to the factories of companies located south of Freienwal-

Overview of the main section of the Soviet restricted area (early 1950)

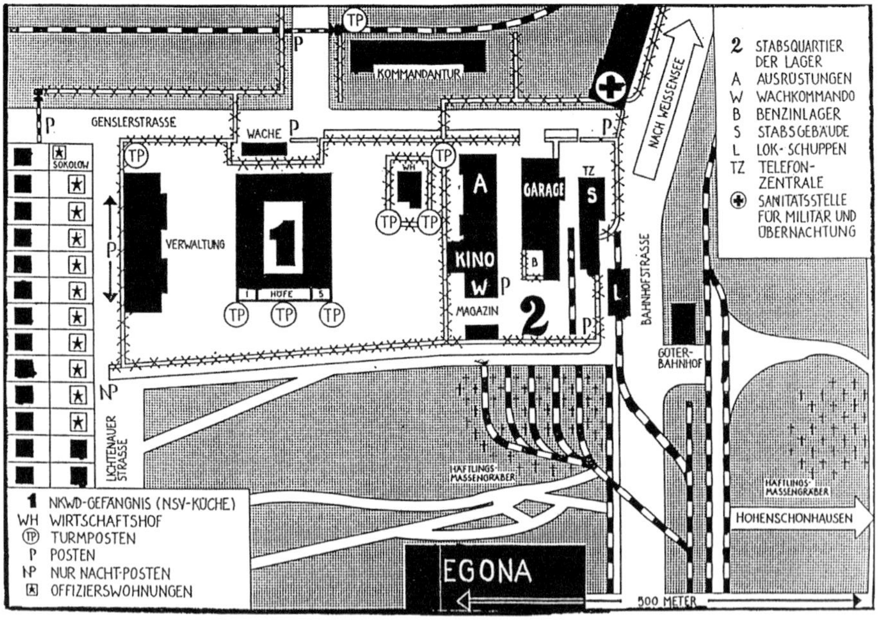

der Strasse, such as "Reiser" and "Barth" at Genslerstrasse 15 and 17/18, no longer had access to the Tegel-Friedrichsfelde industrial railway.

In October 1948 Grosse-Leege-Strasse was probably blocked off at Wriezener Strasse, as well as in front of the entrance to the Kahlbaum factory, which at this point had been transformed into a Soviet limited company. German civilians were not allowed on this street.

With the impoundments of 1947/48 the territorial expansion of the restricted area ended. According to data supplied by the Weissensee district offices, by this point nearly 108,000 square meters of the industrial area had been occupied.

Although the Soviet secret service had hermetically sealed the restricted area off from the beginning, there were individual moments of contact with the outside world in the early days. Prisoners of the Special Camp No. 3, for instance, tried in the summer and fall of 1945 to inform their family members of their location and situation via secret messages. Wives and mothers, on the other hand, tried to maintain contact and supply the men with food and clothing. With persistence on the part of the women or good-naturedness or bribability on the part of the guards, eye contact or a short conversation at the compound fence was possible in exceptional situations. Civilian farm workers and officers from the Special Camp No. 3 sometimes even delivered news and packages. Most of the prisoners in the Special Camp No. 3, however, were unable to send information to the outside world – for their family members they remained missing for months or years.

Only once, on September 16, 1945, did the camp doors open for a brief moment. For unknown reasons those responsible decided to let prisoners' family members visit. Some of these visitors had heard about the event through word of mouth. A large crowd gathered in front of the entrance on Freienwalder Strasse, mostly women and children. For hours the names of the camp prisoners were read off. Family members could then enter the special area individually and advance to Genslerstrasse, while

Encounter at Camp Gate

In front of us, in the fog, is a large factory complex, surrounded by a high iron fence. To the right and left of the entrance are shacks, in front of these Russian guards. A group of women stand at a slight distance, crowded together and shivering. When they recognize me, they approach me and greet me, asking if I hope to see my husband – and if I could give him a piece of paper, a package or a piece of clothing. […] It is already getting dark. One can't see ten meters in the distance and Götz is shaking a bit. He is excited. He is to see his father again, who left the house in June and never returned. I have never brought him to the camp. Why did I do so today? There – he appears out of nowhere! He approaches us with long strides. The little one throws his arms around his neck. – In five minutes we say the most important things to each other and exchange our letters. We take care of the wishes of the women who crowd around us. Then he squeezes my hand and goes back.

Report by the actress Berta Drews about the last meeting between Götz and Heinrich George at the camp gate in Berlin-Hohenschönhausen on December 6, 1945.
Source: Berta Drews: Wohin des Wegs. Erinnerungen. Munich, 1987, pgs. 246–249.

the prisoners had to march forward in blocks or in rows of six. Right in front of the actual camp brief encounters took place – often amidst tears.

In the hope of catching at least a glimpse or another sign of life, the prisoners' families gathered in front of the entrance to the restricted area in the days and weeks that followed. Some may have expected another "visitation day." The inhabitants of the building at Freienwalder Strasse 20 filed a complaint on October 6, 1945 at the 287th police station at Schöneicher Strasse 3–4, saying that a crowd of people gathered everyday in front of their building, people who wanted to visit their family members in the Russian detention camp. "Because of this our apartment building has become a continuous trouble spot. Women try to hide in the house near the Russian guards. All the tenants plead for help because they are afraid for themselves because of the official attack by members of the Red Army against Nazi women."

It never came to a second "visitation day." After several prisoners managed to escape from the Special Camp No. 3 and the neighboring prison labour camp, the director of the Special Camp Department, Colonel Swiridow, ordered the guard personnel on November 26, 1945 to intensify their duties. The few remaining "liberties" with regard to the prisoners' freedom of movement and the possibility of having contact with the outside were abolished.

Despite extensive self-supply and intensified isolation, however, the restricted area was not a self-sufficient entity. It depended on the communal administration structures for its supply of electricity, water and building materials. Representatives from German agencies or businesses were only rarely allowed to enter the restricted area, for example in case of urgent repairs or averages.

In 1949 the isolation was finally somewhat relaxed. Only following the dissolution of the prison labour camp (HAL) in late 1948/early 1949 and the incorporation of the site into the Soviet Administrative Service, were employees of the Berlin water department and garbage collection, as

▷ *The restricted area on a detail of a Soviet aerial photo (early 1950s)*

well as employees of single German workshops, allowed to enter this part of the compound.

After the establishment of the GDR on October 7, 1949 a new period began in the restricted area in Hohenschönhausen. The Soviet occupying power gradually scaled down its administration apparatus, including its security forces operating in Germany. On November 5, 1949 the government of the USSR replaced the Soviet Military Administration in Germany (SMAD) with the less directly present Soviet Control Commission (SCC). The Soviet forces abandoned many buildings in Berlin and their remaining facilities were concentrated in the headquarters in Berlin-Karlshorst. After the camp was closed the responsible department in Hohenschönhausen ceased its activities in April 1950. In July the Soviet Ministry of State Security dissolved its operative department in Berlin and in the spring of 1951 the Soviet Union gave up the restricted military area completely. By this point the site had already lost most of its importance as the headquarters of the Soviet police and secret service authority.

The persecution of political offences was, of course, not over. More and more, responsible for this was rather the GDR's Ministry of State Security (MfS), which had been created in February 1950 and was now to assume the responsibilities of the Soviet security body. It soon needed facilities with the capacity necessary to accommodate its remand prisoners and additional logistical activities. The SCC, therefore, turned the restricted military area in Hohenschönhausen over to the GDR government, effective March 1, 1951, which shortly thereafter made it available to the State Security Service.

Under the Administration of the State Security Service (1951–1990)

The MfS took over the area sometime in the early summer of 1951. The prison building at Genslerstrasse 66 now served as the GDR State Security Service's central remand prison (UHA) and the respective MfS employees moved into the former offices of the Soviet interrogators and guards. In addition to the UHA, headed by high commissioner Hans Bialas since October 1951, the direction and the majority of the workers from the MfS Departments XIV and IX, which were responsible for the remand and imprisonment, as well as for all kinds of criminal investigations, also resided on the site of the former canteen.

At that time the State Security Service was still being developed. As of mid 1952 it was provided with direct guidance from Soviet instructors, so-called advisors. Thereafter, not only did members of the MfS work in Hohenschönhausen during the 1950s, but an unknown number of Soviet secret service employees as well. They had access to all documents and were authorized to give instructions to their MfS coworkers.

The Soviet Ministry of State Security (MGB) inspected the MfS's investigative work very carefully and the instructors themselves handled important cases. Until 1953 they also conducted interrogations and were allowed to have any prisoners who interested them transferred to the Soviet remand prison in Berlin-Karlshorst whenever they wished. For this reason many people believed the prison in Hohenschönhausen to be a cooperative facility of both the MfS and the MGB.

Until 1952 the Soviet secret service in Hohenschönhausen was also allowed to round up convoys of prisoners to be deported to the USSR, initially at the railway

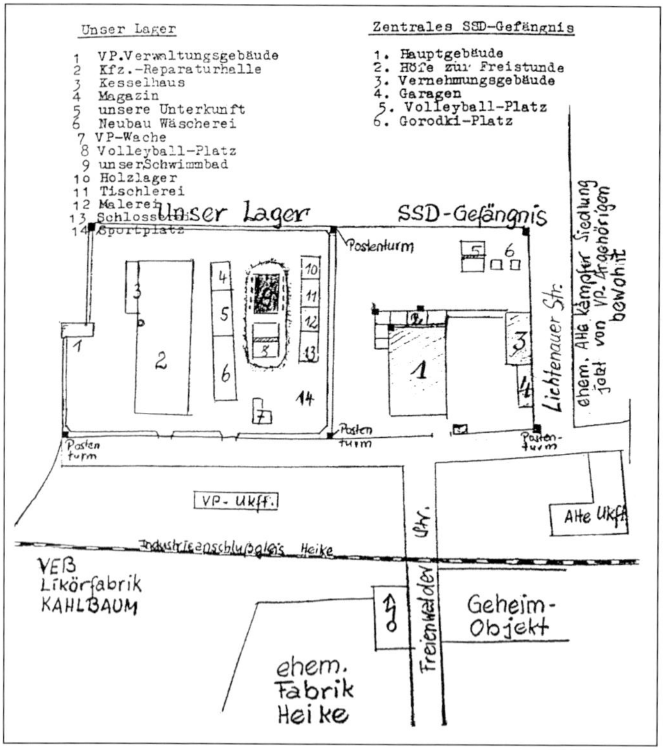

Sketch of camp layout by Werner Sauerzweig, prisoner in Camp X (1954)

siding at Genslerstrasse 69–72, and then by the tracks of the industrial train station. Herded together in box cars that were disguised as blue mail cars from the outside, many Germans, as well as convicted members of the Soviet army, were sent from here to the forced labour camps of the Gulag.

The borders of the restricted area remained virtually unchanged during this period. The only piece of property that was eliminated from the restricted area was the lot belonging to the former Company for Rust Protection at Bahnhofstrasse 7–9. The special zone now comprised areas and buildings at Freienwalder Strasse 6–23, Genslerstrasse 13–17 and 66–72, Goeckestrasse 39–42, Grosse-Leege-Strasse 17a–25 and 95–96, Lichtenauer Strasse 2–24 and Schöneicher Strasse 8–11b, as well as Wriezener Strasse 10–11. The relevant roads remained blocked off by wooden fences and barriers and were inaccessible to public through traffic. Only the industrial train was once again granted permission to pass through the special zone when necessary and to fulfill the transport needs of the remaining businesses located along the dead end track.

The buildings in the restricted area were in dreadful condition when they were taken over by the MfS. A large number of the structures, particularly the tenements, were very run down after being empty for months or rendered unusable because of looting by withdrawing Soviet secret security forces. With the exception of the remand prison, which was obviously turned over to the MfS "in full operation," the buildings had to first be brought back into working order. The MfS deployed inmates from GDR prisons for repair and restoration work, as well as reconstruction measures and new constructions. As of December 1952 they were housed in a prison labour camp, Labour Camp X, located at Genslerstrasse 69–72.

Additional departments of the State Security Service moved into the restricted area after the work was completed. The Main Department of Personal Security (PS) took over most of the other buildings because the number of their personnel had grown so quickly. Its administration was housed in the office building of the former "Heike Factory" at Freienwalder Strasse 17–19 before it was transferred to Berlin-Weissensee. Service departments, which developed secret service equipment and instruments, were housed on the opposite side of the street in the building complex with the house numbers 9–12, in which Aachen Mirror Manufacturer had once produced its goods.

Also situated in the restricted area since 1952 was the "brain" behind the State Security Service: Department XII (information/processing/statistics) with the main index card file on individuals and the affiliated archives. The core of the MfS's future

External wooden fence of restricted area (1956)

central archives were the files that were transferred from the political police (Commissariat 5) in the Soviet zone of occupation. Documents from the Nazi period were also returned from the USSR in railway cars between 1951 and 1959. The file material was initially stored in the former Berthoty wire factory at Genslerstrasse 13, where a small staff of six men and two women worked under the direction of Captain Lieselotte Behrendt. In the early 1960s the archives moved into the former "Heike Factory."

During the 1950s and 1960s the restricted area was enlarged above all to the east and west under the auspices of the State Security Service. The area was extended between the industrial train station and Lichtenauer Strasse all the way to Arendsweg. Between 1959 and 1960a completely new remand prison was erected there.

Preparations for the construction of the new prison in the restricted area of Hohenschönhausen began sometime around 1955. The cause for the decision was probably the popular uprising of June 17, 1953, when over 13,000 people were arrested in the GDR within a few days and whose secure custody had caused great problems. The number of cells in the "U-Boot" ("the submarine") and in the other remand prisons was not sufficient for the State Security Service, leading to the step-by-step enlargement of the remand centers.

The planned site for the new prison in Hohenschönhausen was a lot located behind the "U-Boot" that the MfS used as a garden and sports facility. On November 25, 1955 a positive building lot evaluation was granted by the GDR State Geological Commission. The project then went through different planning phases. The building team 114 of the neighboring Camp X drew up the first

Entrance gateway of prison (photo from November 1990)

detailed construction drawings for the new building – internally referred to as "HV addition" – in 1956/57. Already in its preliminary design the building contained its rectangular U-shaped form although originally it was only to be two stories high. The northern and southern wings were to be connected to the existing prison in the former National Socialist People's Welfare Organization (NSV) canteen via corridors in the basement and upper story. In the courtyard there was to be a star-shaped day release cell facility with a guard post in the middle. Aside from the technical facilities, administration and housekeeping rooms, as well as sanitary and supply facilities in the basement and on the ground floor, the building plans for all wings showed nothing but cells. Prisoners were also to occupy the basement in the building section to the south.

In 1958 the responsible parties in the MfS then decided to erect a three-story structure with a cell wing and an interrogation wing. Originally construction was to begin in 1957 but, in fact, was delayed until the first half of 1959. Finally 250 prisoners from Camp X constructed the building. Plans were continually altered, even during the construction phase. For example, the nursery with green houses that had been included in the plans from 1959 and that was to be built on Arendsweg at the corner of Lichtenauer Strasse was never constructed. The prison's day release facility was not built either.

Control room in the north wing of the prison (photo from November 1990)

Daily Life in the Cell

We woke at 5:00 in the morning. We had to get out of the wooden beds and then a washbowl was put in the cell. After that the hatch opened and a hose with water coming out was put in that we had to catch in our washbowl. In the mornings a roll with margarine or jam was handed through the hatch, at noon a bowl with soup, in the evening four meager rolls again. The cell was dreary and gray, the windows bricked up with glass bricks. You couldn't open the window and you couldn't see outside. There was only an airshaft. During my detention it was absolutely forbidden to lie down and to write or read during the day.

Sigrid Paul, divorced, married name Rührdanz, was arrested in February 1963 for "assisting an escape" and was in detention until August of the same year in Berlin-Hohenschönhausen.
Source: Maria Nooke: Der Verratene Tunnel. Geschichte einer verhinderten Flucht im geteilten Berlin. Bremen, 2002, pg. 99.

A repair area for trucks and buses was created in the first half of the 1960s on the compound near Arendsweg. The prisoners of Camp X were to carry out the work in two shed-roofed halls, arranged in an L. To heat the restricted area the MfS's Main Department of Administration and Economy had an oil heating plant with a two-story structure for the boiler and a fifty-meter high smoke stack built to the east of the labour camp. The tank container was supplied with heating oil by rail. In the mid 1960s the small residential area on the southern side of Lichtenauer Strasse was enlarged. The MfS incorporated four additional properties here (No. 26–32) into the restricted area.

In order to accommodate their many employees, the State Security Service had several new buildings constructed in the western part of the restricted area. At Goeckestrasse 40–42 and in the vicinity of Grosse-Leege-Strasse 20–25 prisoners from Camp X erected six buildings with 230 apartments between 1953 and 1958. At the end of the 1950s, however, the MfS eliminated all the apartment buildings in the Goeckestrasse and to the west of the Grosse-Leege-Strasse, as well as the garage complex in the Schöneicher Strasse, from the restricted area. This was done for administrative and security reasons, since family members also lived in the buildings and had to go to work or school on a regular basis. The restrictive measures and ban on through traffic was largely repealed in this area.

MfS architecture in the 1970s was characterized by prefabricated buildings of precast concrete elements and hall-type structures. Such buildings were also erected within the restricted area, for example in 1972/73 at Freienwalder Strasse 14 for Department N (communication) and at Genslerstrasse 13 for the Operative Technical Sector (OTS). Prisoners from Camp X no longer participated in the construction work. These tasks were initially carried out by the Ministry's state-owned construction company, the VEB Montage-Bau-Berlin (MBB) and, from 1975 on, by the state-owned company for special structural engineering, the VEB Spezialhochbau Berlin (SHB).

Main Department IX, responsible for criminal investigations, was primarily housed together until then with Department XIV,

Storage area of the Department of Behind the Lines Services on Freienwalder, at the corner of Grosse-Leege-Strasse (April 1976)

responsible for MfS remand prisons, in the former canteen. In 1973 these departments moved into new offices in the Lichtenauer Strasse, located in a six-story building (Building 50 B). The investigation department was enlarged again in the years that followed and occupied several buildings in this area.

In the first half of the 1970s the restricted area grew in other areas. The increasing need for secret service devices and equipment led to the expansion of the responsible department, the OTS. The external security also needed to be improved. The State Security Service, therefore, decided to incorporate a strip of land to the west of Genslerstrasse 14–15 and 17 and a part of the property at Goeckestrasse 37–38. In 1972 the Main Department of Administration and Economy drafted plans for the construction of several office buildings with approximately 1,000 work places, a 1,600 square meter large production area and 3,000 square meters of storage space. There were also plans for a "full kitchen for 2,000 meals" to feed all the employees in the entire restricted area. The prerequisite for this was that the businesses and facilities on the site would be transferred elsewhere and that these spaces would be made available. MfS planners estimated that about eighty million East German marks would be needed to erect the building and all necessary secondary structures. Preparations were begun to accommodate part of the engineering services (heating and telephone).

The tracks of the industrial railway were also included in the businesses and facilities to be moved away or disassembled. Following the construction of the Berlin Wall, the activity radius of the Tegel-Friedrichsfelde industrial railway became more and more constrained. In the early seventies the MfS brought about the withdrawal of the permit to operate the sidings behind the Werneu-

Dead-end tracks of the industrial rail in the restricted area (April 1976)

chener Strasse. The administration of the East German Railway proved to be a tough negotiating partner. Only after enforcing the law passed on September 20, 1961 pertaining to the defense of the GDR could the tracks and switches between the Bahnhof- and Werneuchener Strasse actually be removed in the late 1970s. On May 31, 1983 the MfS was finally registered in the cadastre as the new legal owner of the land.

During the 1980s new building activities were concentrated on this recently acquired land. The planned office canteen, as well as the offices and storage space for the OTS, were built along the former railway line between Gensler- and Goeckestrasse. A special building was also erected to house the data center of Department XIII (central data processing center) and of the Main Administration for Reconnaissance (HV A).

Under the auspices of the MfS not only was the restricted area enlarged and numerous new buildings erected, but external security was also perfected. Following the take over of the restricted area by the MfS in 1951, the security measures functioned at a relatively primitive level. The wooden barriers and the electric alarm provisions, as well as the wire fences and the areas guarded by unleashed German shepherds, were

Aerial photo of the restricted area. Both dormitory buildings for singles in foreground (November / October 1988)

Watch tower post no. 5 at the corner of Lichtenauer / Gensler-strasse (March 1988)

primarily designed to keep unauthorized people from entering the compound and to thwart prisoners' escape attempts. The guards were also mainly trained to deal with such tasks. In the 1950s, however, it was entirely possible to approach the site and to observe it, as a series of contemporary photographs taken at that time and published in West Germany demonstrate.

The external security of the secret service complex was initially incumbent on a command of the Berlin Guard Regiment (WR). Very few MfS employees in the restricted area were actually armed. Until the popular uprising of June 17, 1953, the idea of storming party headquarters, MfS offices and remand centers was totally beyond the imagination of SED leaders. It was only after the shock of those protests that the responsible parties decided to employ additional security measures. A more detailed alarm and defense plan was established that same year. The plan was based on three danger levels and specified how the security forces should proceed in situations of "serious provocations, armed attacks and attempted or executed acts of sabotage, as well as other threatening dangers." In the case of the highest alarm level (III) the complete defense of the entire compound was organized by a central command post via four military bases. In cases of emergency the restricted area Freienwalder- / Genslerstrasse was to be included in a defense system with the second restricted area in Hohenschönhausen as an additional "node of resistance."

Provisions for the "S-scenario" were updated on a regular basis and adjusted to the actual situation. The MfS continued to replace the wooden fences and watchtowers with structures made of brick and concrete and supplemented the electric security technology with surveillance cameras.

A comprehensive security plan for the secret compound, however, was first implemented in the 1960s. Fundamental to this was an elaborately designed system of entry and the systematic isolation of the individual departments within the restricted area. The plan also included visual shields and outer perimeter security systems to ensure that the area was not observed from outside. To this end a network of MfS residential and office buildings was created. This included the official residences at Grosse-Leege-Strasse 17a–25, Goeckestrasse 37a–42b and at Werneuchener Strasse 21a–e, as well as both of the MfS's dormitories for single people at Genslerstrasse 18 and Werneuchener Strasse 19. At Grosse-Leege-Strasse 97–98 the state-owned technical security company, the VEB Sicherheitstechnik, subordinate to the MfS supply services, bordered directly on the "administrative bureau in the Freienwalder Strasse."

The building complex at Grosse-Leege-Strasse 101–103 created the northern section of the shield ring, which included the administrative headquarters of the Department of Behind the Line Services (VRD)

Restricted area border fence with surveillance camera at Genslerstrasse (March 1988)

and by the work premises of the state-owned special structural engineering company, The VEB Spezialhochbau Berlin, at Gärtnerstrasse 15–18. The construction management department of the MfS also had dwellings and workshops located at Genslerstrasse 14–15 and 17. Task Force XVII (West Berlin visitor's bureau) and the Main Department XXII (terror defense) had their offices towards the southeast, at Lichtenauer Strasse 42–50 and Ferdinand-Schulze-Strasse 55–71. It was here that the new MfS district office for Hohenschönhausen was being built at the end of the 1980s.

The counterespionage department was also responsible for the external surveillance of the restricted area. Main Department II/21 recorded individuals they saw roaming the area with cameras checking on workers, who had to make repairs in the buildings. Beginning in the 1960s the department also monitored the residents in the Bahnhof- and Genslerstrasse, as well as on Lichtenauer, Lössauer and Schleizer Strasse. People who had "western contacts" were investigated with particular care. Investigations were conducted after the fact on "republic fugitives" and who had lived in one of these streets and left the GDR illegally. The department could also depend on voluntary informers and their own "unofficial" informers (IM) for their investigations of the residents.

When a multi-story residential building was erected near the restricted area, counterespionage specialists investigated whether it was possible to look into or photograph the compound from it. Assisted by the Municipal District Administration, they then had buildings classified as "moving-in-restricted" and only MfS employees or other confidants were able to live on the floors in question.

There were fewer options for action against the activities of the British, French or American military missions. Equipped with unusual powers resulting from the special allied status they were granted after the Second World War, their employees were able to drive their vehicles right up to the restricted area and observe the area and

Members of the western military mission at the entrance to the Motor Vehicle Services area on Bahnhofstrasse (1980s)

take pictures. The MfS, who provoked accidents at other locations to scare off the western observers, however, watched them in the process.

In 1970s the MfS had planned to incorporate additional areas into the restricted area in order to close the gaps in the external security ring. These and other measures could not be realized, however, because the massive protests by the GDR population brought an unexpected end to the SED regime in 1989/90.

After the Fall of the Wall

Following the dismissal of Party Leader and Head of State Erich Honecker on October 18, 1989, the new GDR government headed by Hans Modrow pasted two resolutions granting political prisoners amnesty. Prisoners who had been arrested for or convicted of trying to escape from the GDR, subversive agitation or similar offenses were released from prison in November and December.

The fall of the Berlin Wall on November 9 led to signs of dissolution in MfS departments in Hohenschönhausen. Members of the State Security Service quit the service and tried to find new jobs or went into early retirement. Particularly in the technical departments of the VRD and the OTS, strategies were quickly developed on how certain parts of the departments could be transferred to civilian scientific and service areas.

After the State Security Service was permanently dissolved, the GDR government transferred a series of responsibilities and facilities, which had been in the hands of the State Security Service until then, to the Ministry of the Interior (MdI). In the restricted area Hohenschönhausen this included the prison hospital of the Central medical Service (ZMD) and the former Department N (communication). The MdI also appointed the so-called area's facility commander. Most important, however, was its takeover of the heart of the secret district: the State Security Service's central remand prison.

The prison was now filled with completely different prisoners: leading GDR government and party functionaries, such as the union leader head Harry Tisch, the CDU chairman, Gerald Götting, and the top economic advisor, Günter Mittag, all of whom were arrested and sent to Hohenschönhausen. Under pressure from the furious population and in order to clear themselves, the GDR courts carried out investigations concerning these men for abuse of office, cronyism and squandering of public property. Even the dismissed Minister of State Security was twice arrested and accused by the public prosecutor's office of being responsible for the prosecution of political dissidents and for providing members of the terrorist Red Army Fraction (RAF) with refuge. Like an irony of history, he was imprisoned in early 1990 in the prison complex he had created – in Cell 11 of the prison hospital. He pronounced himself sick in order to avoid being held legally accountable for his actions.

The dismissed SED functionaries encountered much better prison conditions than the MfS's former remand prisoners

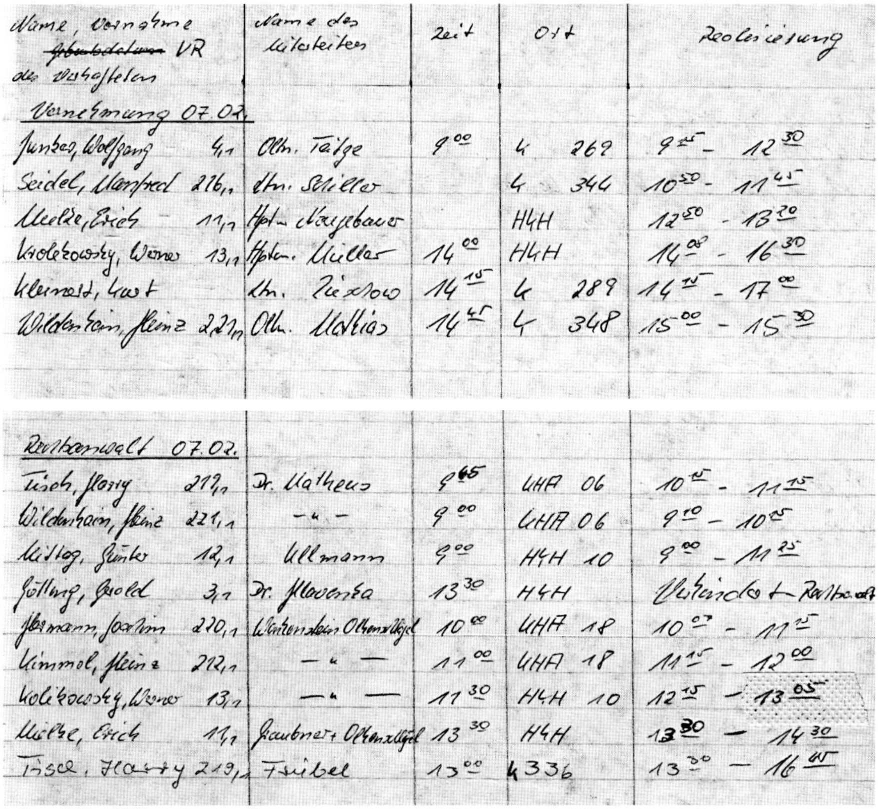

Name, Vorname ~~Geburtsdatum~~ VR des Verhafteten	Name des Mitarbeiters	Zeit	Ort	Realisierung
Vernehmung 07.02.				
Junker, Wolfgang 4,1	Oltn. Teige	9^{00}	4 262	9^{15} - 12^{30}
Seidel, Manfred 216,1	Ltn. Schiller		4 344	10^{50} - 11^{45}
Mielke, Erich 11,1	Hptm. Neugebauer		H4H	12^{50} - 13^{20}
Krolikowsky, Werner 13,1	Hptm. Müller	14^{00}	H4H	14^{08} - 16^{30}
Kleinert, Kurt	Ltn. Zieslow	14^{15}	4 289	14^{15} - 17^{00}
Wildenhain, Heinz 221,1	Oltn. Mathias	14^{45}	4 348	15^{00} - 15^{30}
Rechtsanwalt 07.02.				
Tisch, Harry 219,1	Dr. Matheus	9^{45}	UHA 06	10^{15} - 11^{15}
Wildenhain, Heinz 221,1	-"-	9^{00}	UHA 06	9^{10} - 10^{05}
Mittag, Günter 12,1	Ullmann	9^{00}	H4H 10	9^{00} - 11^{25}
Götting, Gerald 3,1	Dr. Hlavenka	13^{30}	H4H	Verhindert Rechtsanwalt
Herrmann, Joachim 220,1	Wintersdorf Oltn. Vogel	10^{00}	UHA 18	10^{07} - 11^{15}
Kimmel, Heinz 212,1	-"-	11^{00}	UHA 18	11^{15} - 12^{00}
Kolikowsky, Werner 13,1	-"-	11^{30}	H4H 10	12^{15} - 13^{05}
Mielke, Erich 11,1	Jaubner + Oltn. Vogel	13^{30}	H4H	13^{30} - 14^{30}
Tisch, Harry 219,1	Friebel	13^{00}	4336	13^{30} - 16^{45}

Excerpt from the summons book of the remand prison from February 7, 1990

had: In the cells spring-mounted beds replaced the ones of wood, several custody rooms on the second floor of the east wing were given windows and rooms for visitors were provided for the first time on the ground floor of the interrogation section. Behind the new prison building most of the partitions between the free access cells were demolished, so that three large outdoor spaces with seating and flower boxes were created. The temporary inmates in the prison hospital, Erich Mielke and Harry Tisch, were even allowed to spend their free time in the prison courtyard, which was embellished with beds of roses and benches, something that no prisoner would ever have set eyes on during the MfS period.

Portions of the buildings in the restricted military area were taken over by other institutions. The GDR government, for instance, made arrangements on January 13, 1990 for the OTS's development and production workshops and the remaining MfS specialists to be allocated to the Ministry of Science and Technology. The vehicles from the supply and truck service garage were transferred to the Service Combine (later called the Technical Service and Distribution GmbH) and to the state-owned Autoservice Berlin (today CSB, Car Service Berlin GmbH).

The building at Freienwalder Strasse 17–19, in which the MfS stored a secret Nazi archive, became the branch office of the GDR Central Archives. The national committee for the dissolution of the Agency for National Security (AfNS) transferred the MfS apartment blocks near the restricted area over to the communal apartment administration or, in the case of the dormitory

View of the remand prison and investigation division (photo from November 1990)

for single people at Genslerstrasse 18 and Werneuchener Strasse 19, to other civilian users. In mid May 1990 the council of the district Berlin-Hohenschönhausen had the barriers torn down. Freienwalder- and Genslerstrasse were again freely accessible for the first time in more than forty years.

The reunification of the two German states on October 3, 1990 brought about the final dissolution of the restricted area. On October 1 at 13:00 the MdI handed over the keys to the remand center to the Berlin Senate Administration for Justice. Probably the facility's last prisoner, Erich Mielke was transferred on October 4, 1990 to the Correctional Facility Moabit. The prison was closed down at the end of the month. After this it only served as a storage facility for the central files of the GDR penal system that contained nearly 700,000 files on almost all the people who had been arrested between 1950 and 1990.

The other buildings went to the trust institution for the administration of former GDR property, which gradually sold or transferred them to new owners and to tenants who opened stores or offered other services in them. Many new businesses established in the first half of the 1990s, however, did not survive long. Financial straits forced even the district offices of Hohenschönhausen to move out of the buildings on Freienwalder Strasse that the administration had occupied.

Other structures that characterized the appearance of the restricted area until 1989 were demolished. The watchtowers and the guardhouses on Freienwalder Strasse have disappeared, as have the MfS oil heating plant and many facilities of the former department for motor vehicle maintenance. The enormous main production hall of the "Heike Factory," which had existed since the beginning of the district's industrial development, was leveled in 2003. The former remand center was made a national landmark in 1992 and, additionally, has been a memorial site since 1995.

The Departments

The Hohenschönhausen restricted area was much more than just a central remand prison. A number of very different departments of the State Security Service resided here, many of which reported directly to Erich Mielke, Minister of State Security. In addition to the central units, which were responsible for criminal prosecution and imprisonment, a number of mostly technical and support departments also had their offices on the expansive grounds. A total of at least 2,500 people worked here for the Ministry of State Security (MfS).

Prison Administration

Department XIV of the MfS worked in the former canteen until early 1990. This department, which employed 255 full-time staff members in 1989, was the State Security Services' central prison administration and was responsible for the security of all MfS prisons.

In the early years of the Ministry of State Security, these tasks were handled by the remand subdivision within Department IX, which was responsible for criminal proceedings. In 1951, however, the subdivision was removed from this department and established as an independent department of its own directly subordinate to the Minister of State Security. From 1952 to 1958 the department was headed by the former electrician Paul Rumpelt, who was later succeeded by the one-time drainage worker Hans Bialas. In 1963 Siegfried Rataizik, a trained plumber, was at its head and remained in this position until the MfS was dissolved. The lieutenant colonel, who received a doctorate degree in 1984 from the MfS Law School in Potsdam, directed the MfS prison administration for 27 years.

The most important task of Department XIV was overseeing the security of Remand Prison I in Berlin-Hohenschönhausen. The uniformed wardens conducted body searches on prisoners upon their arrival,

List of weapons of different State Security divisions in restricted area (1954)

1954

BStU
000057

Zur Verfügung stehende Waffen:

Objekt I :	7	M Pi	98o Schuß	
	11	Mauser	477 Schuß	
	15	Pistolen 7.65	28o Schuß	
	5	Pistolen 0.8	2oo Schuß	
	7	Karabiner	287 Schuß	
	8	Pistolen 7.65	56 Schuß	(ständige Waffentr.)
	53	Waffen	2 88o Schuß	
Objekt St.V.:	2o	P 38	28o Schuß	
	5	Mauser	3oo Schuß	
	2	Walter	14 Schuß	
	1	Mauser befindet sich in Reparatur		
	27	Waffen	594 Schuß	
Objekt IV :	1	M Pi	14o Schuß	
	2	Mauser	8o Schuß	
	3	Pistolen 0.8	48 Schuß	
	6	Waffen	268 Schuß	
Objekt S :	8	K 98	12o Schuß	
	5	M Pi	7oo Schuß	
	9	P 38	132 Schuß	
	22	Waffen	952 Schuß	
Objekt PS :	4	M Pi	56o Schuß	und 48o Reserve
	2o	Mauser	4oo Schuß	und 6oo Reserve
	13	Parabellum	91 Schuß	
	37	Waffen	1 o51 Schuß	und 1 o8o Reserve

Nights in the Cell

There goes the light again. This time I concentrate on this cursed contraption: There is a square hole right above the door ... with a glass plate in front of it ... reflecting glass or something like it. It has a very bright light bulb attached to it. This contraption can be operated from the outside making almost the entire cell as light as day. You can forget about sleeping. I started counting. "one, two, three, ... four ... five ..." I reach 60, then they start beaming at me again. I continue to count: one, two, three, four – this time I get to 118. But this doesn't help much either. I will never being able to fall asleep like this. But they know that all too well. Why else would they do it in such short intervals? I turn over onto my side and pull the blanket over my head. It is not long before I hear rattling, the hatch is pulled down and a young, rather fat woman in uniform screams at me in dialect: "Get your hands off the blanket. And lie on your back!" Horror-stricken, I obey.

Ellen Thiemann was arrested in December 1972 for attempting to cross the border illegally. She was held in remand in Berlin-Hohenschönhausen until mid-June 1973.
Source: Ellen Thiemann: Stell dich mit den Schergen gut. Erinnerungen an die DDR. Meine Wiederbegegnung mit dem Zuchthaus Hoheneck. Munich / Berlin 1990, p. 30.

locked them in their cells, shoved the meals through the hatch in the cell door and escorted prisoners to their interrogation. They also controlled the labour commandos in Berlin-Hohenschönhausen, which consisted of convicted prisoners who were forced to do cleaning, cooking and repair chores for the MfS.

Department XIV also managed the other central MfS prison, Remand Prison II in Berlin-Lichtenberg. This prison on Magdalenenstrasse came into frequent use in the

Former "U-Boot" ("the submarine") and later administration building of Division XIV (photo from November 1990)

sixties when prisoners were granted permission to speak with a lawyer, embassy employee or relative. They were brought here for these meetings so that it would not be necessary for outsiders to enter the restricted area Hohenschönhausen.

For almost two decades the department was also responsible for Camp X, where convicted prisoners were forced to do labour for the MfS. The camp, which existed until 1974, was situated right next to the remand prison in Hohenschönhausen. This department also supervised the work of fifteen regional remand prisons in the district capitals of the German Democratic Republic until the MfS was dissolved. It drew up the annual task plans, issued instructions and checked that they were implemented. The department also oversaw prisoner transports abroad. Refugees who were captured at the borders of friendly states such as Hungary or Bulgaria were flown back to the German Democratic Republic, accompanied by a department employee. The department also saw to it that the cars left behind by refugees were transported back to the GDR.

Central Investigation Department

Since 1973, the headquarters of Main Department IX, the Central Investigation Department of the MfS, had been located in a six-story prefabricated building set behind the remand prison. More than any other department of the State Security Service, the MfS investigative organ was directly involved in the persecution of people involved in opposition and resistance. The department was founded in 1950 and promoted to the level of a main department in 1953. Unlike other secret services, the MfS had not only police powers, but also prosecuting jurisdiction through its main department. It functioned as a "Socialist administrative organ of justice" – a practice that was not officially set in law until 1968. The Investigation Department, which in the end had a staff of 484 workers, also reported directly to Mielke, who was also a member of its SED founding organization. The main department also supervised the work of the investigative departments of the State Security Service's fifteen local authority areas.

Investigation Department offices on Lichtenauer Strasse (photo from 1998)

The so-called Line IX was responsible for all criminal proceedings in the German Democratic Republic entailing crimes believed to be politically significant – regardless of whether GDR citizens or foreigners were involved. It investigated crimes such as "subversive agitation," "attempted escape from the Republic," "assaults on the state border," "human trade," "illegal contacts" and "treason." Clauses of the penal code allowed for all political dissention to be regarded as a crime. In the eighties anyone who publicly "vilified" the state or the work of GDR state organs could be sentenced to up to two years imprisonment.

The Investigation Department was also responsible for investigating general crimes, which bore a political nature. These included cases of murder, manslaughter, fire or damage, which caused considerable injury to the state and crimes, which involved

Months of Solitary Confinement

I was continually interrogated in irregular intervals for four or five months. These irregular interrogations were demoralizing. It is good to see the cell door opened again, to be picked up for an interrogation. I was in solitary confinement for weeks and months, without being allowed to work. Time just doesn't move forward under those circumstances. One day feels as long as fourteen days. When I was really badly off, I would think about the prisoners of war in Russia and say to myself: "These people spent ten, sometimes fourteen years in the Soviet Union under the most horrible circumstances." These thoughts comforted me. To make the situation bearable I would do sports in the cell until I collapsed. I did pushups and ran five thousand meters inside the cell. I would keep running back and forth. The most absurd ideas would come into my head. I created a game out of toilet paper that I rolled into small pieces: five, three, one. You had to take something away from each row. Whoever took away the last piece lost the game. At first I played against myself. Later when I wasn't alone in the cell, I played against other prisoners. Sports and this kind of brain training kept me going.

Uwe Rath was arrested in February of 1963 for providing what was known as "escape aid." He was in the Berlin-Hohenschönhausen remand prison until August of that year.
Source: Maria Nooke: Der Verratene Tunnel. Geschichte einer verhinderten Flucht im geteilten Berlin. Bremen, 2002, pgs. 78/79.

members of the State Security Service, the Nationale Volksarmee (National People's Army) or Soviet military forces and other instances. The department also handled Nazi and war crimes. And finally, it oversaw the Bautzen II special prison, where many of the prisoners from Hohenschönhausen were transferred to after they were convicted.

During its forty years of existence, Line IX carried out 90,000 pre-trial investigations, many of which ended in a conviction. The main department not only conducted investigations, it also prepared the criminal proceedings. In many cases it had a direct influence on the trial and the final sentence. Especially in the fifties it staged numerous show trials against opponents of the SED leadership. The trials were designed to make an impression on the public. Cases deemed special or involving a prominent prisoner often led department officials to seek the approval of the SED leadership before determining the sentence.

In the first half of the fifties, the Investigation Department was headed by the former druggist Alfred Scholz. In 1956 the position was filled by the one-time metal machinist Kurt Richter. The trained orchestra musician Walter Heinitz took over the post in 1964 and was succeeded in 1973 by the zincographer Rolf Fister. Fister, who received a doctorate degree in law from the MfS Law School in 1975, headed the department until it was closed down at the beginning of 1990.

Medical Service

Some sections of the Ministry of State Security's Central Medical Service (ZMD) were located on the grounds of the remand prison. In 1974 this center was responsible for treating and evaluating prisoners in the prison hospital. Prisoners who fell ill were brought to the MfS' own staff doctors in order to prevent any information from leaking to the outside. The Medical Service was also responsible for the medical care of the Security Service staff.

In the fifties the State Security Service hired independent doctors under contract, but by 1959 it had created its own medical care structure – probably in response to the exposure of the dentist Gerhard Raue, who had passed on information about MfS employees and high-level functionaries from the government hospital. The ZMD, which was created from the Medical Department in 1974, was henceforth responsible for all medical tasks.

The ZMD provided basic medical care – everything from eye exams to dental treatment – to all full-time State Security staff. It also provided medical and psychological counseling to MfS members involved or preparing for a special assignment. Unofficial informers (IM) and undercover officers on special assignment could also receive treatment from the ZMD if needed. For example, Günter Guillaume, an East German spy in the West German federal chancellery, was entrusted to the care of the ZMD doctors after he was released from prison and returned to the GDR.

The ZMD employed 1,161 people in 1989. In addition to the prison hospital in the restricted area, it was also in charge of a number of other medical institutions: a hospital in Berlin-Buch with 260 beds, the polyclinic in the MfS headquarters in Berlin-Lichtenberg, numerous out-patient district stations, the MfS food and water investigation agency and the State Security's general hygiene inspection office. The MfS had its own supply service, which provided these institutions with the necessary medical equipment and products.

The ZMD, which had its main offices on Normannenstrasse in Berlin, was officially part of the Main Department of Cadre und Training. Günter Kempe, who had previously worked for the Ministry of State Security as a contract doctor and who in 1977 received a doctorate degree in 1977 from MfS Law School, became the first director of the Medical Service. After 26 years in this capacity he was succeeded by his deputy, the medical specialist Klaus-Wolfgang Klein, who headed the ZMD until it was dissolved.

Surveillance Technology Production

The department known as the Operative Technical Sector (OTS) of the State Security Service was the largest division in the Hohenschönhausen restricted area. In 1989 1,085 full-time employees worked there. The department's main task was the production of special intelligence technology for the MfS.

In the fifties Department K (development of operative technical means) and Department L (acquisition of operative technical means) were responsible for these activities. In 1960 these two departments were joined together to form a workgroup of the MfS Main Department B (planning). In 1963 the OTS became an independent division and over time other areas were added such as the Department E (operative technical means and documents) in 1985. The trained metalworker Herbert Hentschke served as director until 1967 when he was succeeded by the electronics engineer Günter Schmidt.

The OTS was responsible for the development, production and maintenance of every kind of espionage equipment including secret wiretapping devices, cameras, camouflage and monitoring instruments. The department also made copies of keys for

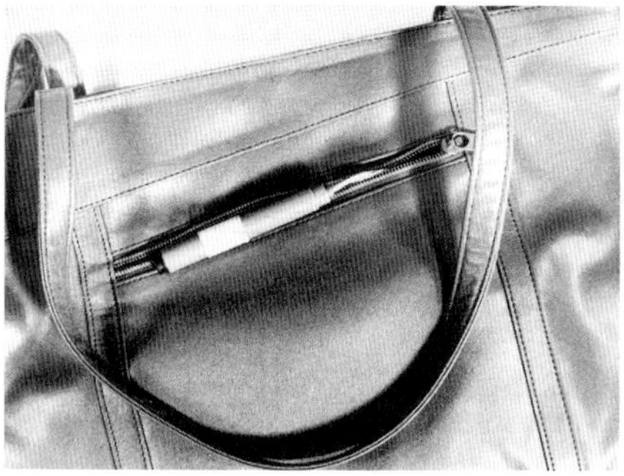

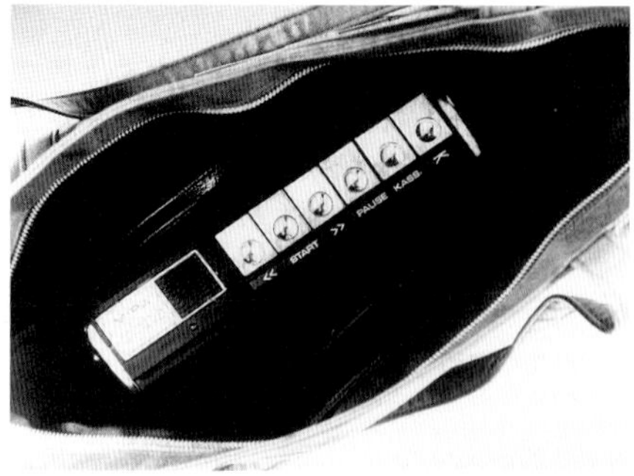

Disguised MfS wire-tapping device. Left: Bag with microphone seen from the outside; right: view into the bag

conspiratorial house searches. Its staff invented devices for the purpose of examining private mail. They could open and reseal letters quickly without leaving a trace. In the eighties one of these machines could open six hundred standard letters per hour. Using this method, 90,000 letters were examined each day throughout the German Democratic Republic.

Base for listening into beam radio routes of the West German Postal Service and radio and car phone communications

The OTS also developed physical, chemical and photographic techniques to recognize hidden information in letters, for example by decoding texts written in cipher. Handwriting analyses and the continually growing OTS fingerprint collection were also important, enabling the State Security Service to identify the writers of hand-made fliers.

The five office buildings of the OTS were equipped with modern laboratories where criminological and scientific experiments could be conducted. Documents and files could be analyzed here and if called for by a secret operation, they could also be reproduced or forged. The OTS had access to western equipment and documents that the MfS had confiscated during arrests. The department evaluated all suggestions for improvement that were submitted to the MfS Central Office of Enhancement. The Institute for Technical Experiments (ITU), which was located outside the restricted area, addressed special issues involving radio defense, wire-tapping technology and electronic data processing. With the help of the OTS, the MfS was able to infiltrate the West German telephone system and a large part of the radio communication, including long-distance transmissions in the eighties. In the end, technical sources had become as important to the GDR espionage as human informers.

The special know-how of OTS made it possible to monitor the entire population of the GDR and also keep surveillance on visitors, journalists and diplomats from the West, for example when they came to the Interhotels. Both wire-tapping devices and video cameras were installed for this purpose. The "made in Hohenschönhausen" equipment was also used by the Soviet KGB and the secret services of other socialist states.

Guard Regiment

The Hohenschönhausen restricted area was guarded by a unit of the Guard Regiment (WR), which worked closely with the facility commander. In 1980, 28 MfS soldiers kept the area under constant surveillance from twelve positions: They consisted of eight watchtowers, one changing position and three security posts at the entrance and exit to the restricted area. The soldiers were routinely armed with pistols and rapid-fire weapons. In an emergency and with the help of additional MfS forces, they were supposed to be able to defend the area against an attack, even one from the outside, in which case they would have hand grenades, anti-tank weapons and armored vehicles at their disposal.

The WR was created from the MfS Guard Battalion that was founded in 1950. It was the military arm of the State Security Service and built up systematically after the popular uprising of June 17, 1953. In 1967 it was named after Feliks Edmundowitsch Dzierzynski, founder of the Soviet secret police, "in recognition of its reliable duty and high-level of readiness." In 1989 the Guard Regiment contained more than 11,000 men, and had thus acquired the strength of an army unit.

In the end, the Guard Regiment consisted of 2,500 professional officers and more than 8,700 regular soldiers. Recruitment was taken care of directly by the Ministry of State Security. Every soldier accepted into its ranks underwent an extensive political and personal examination. Only candidates deemed ideologically reliable were selected. Every sentry swore an oath of allegiance "as a member of the Ministry of State Security, to fight to my death against the enemies of Socialism." The non-commissioned officers volunteered for duty for a period of three years. After their service, many of them were recruited by the MfS as informers (IMs) or full-time employees.

The most important barracks of the regiment were located in Ahrensfelde, Berlin-Adlershof and Erkner. The sentries guarded over a hundred buildings of the MfS, the GDR government and the SED in Greater Berlin. Their training and weapons were designed to enable the soldiers to respond to both a military threat from the outside as well as internal riots. In certain buildings they also controlled passenger traffic in cooperation with the Main Department of Personal Security (PS). They were also involved in official demonstrations and mass events and an honorary company of the Guard Regiment – with orchestra – was present when Erich Honecker, Chairman of the Council of State, received foreign guests and diplomats.

Officially the WR was subordinate to the director of the Ministers Workgroup (AGM). Its immediate head was first the former unskilled labourer Werner Barth (1954–1958) and later the technician surveyor Günter Wolf (1959–1962), both of whom had spent many years in Soviet captivity. In 1962 the qualified dental mechanic Heinz Gronau took charge and was succeeded by the metal machinist and Wehrmacht volunteer Bernd Elsner (1972–1987). The last commander of the Guard Regiment was Manfred Döring, who began his career in the fifties in the GDR's Kasernierte Volkspolizei (People's Police in Barracks).

Armaments Department

The Ministry of State Security had an extensive armaments supply at its disposal. In addition to the more than 200,000 revolvers and machine pistols, it also consisted of 3,611 rifles, 3,537 bazookas, 449 light and 766 heavy machine guns and various armored vehicles. It was supervised by the Armaments Department/Chemical Services Department (BCD), located in the well-guarded restricted area of Hohenschönhausen.

The MfS Armaments Department that was built up in the early fifties was first part of the Department of Communications and later designated Department 7 of the Main Department of Administration and Economy. After the popular uprising of June 17, 1953, the department became responsible for seeing that every MfS staff member received regular lessons in shooting a gun. Later it only conducted training for weapons technicians and chemical protection workers. In the first years most of the MfS weapons were from Germany and had been produced before 1945. By 1958 the ministry began using Soviet makes. In 1961 the department was re-established as the independent Department of Arms and Equipment, and placed under the Ministers Workgroup (AGM). By 1972 it bore the name Department BCD and employed 176 workers in the end.

The department was not only responsible for providing the State Security Service with weapons, ammunition and pioneering technology, it also took care of weapons maintenance. It examined the weapons of "Dynamo," the MfS marksmen sports association, and at some point it also checked the State Security Service's hunting armory.

An additional task entailed providing protection to the MfS from radiation, poison and weapons of mass destruction. The department had an extensive collection of protective equipment available for this purpose. In cooperation with the Central Medical Service (ZMD), its main radiation protection commissioner checked the handling of radioactive materials in the MfS. This included x-ray equipment that was used in the remand prisons for medical purposes and to examine packages. The MfS also used radioactive material to "mark" manuscripts, objects and people and to x-ray cars crossing the border. Through the Department for Special Imports and Storage Rostock II (Object Kavelstorf) it became involved in the GDR's secret arms deals.

In the sixties the department was run by

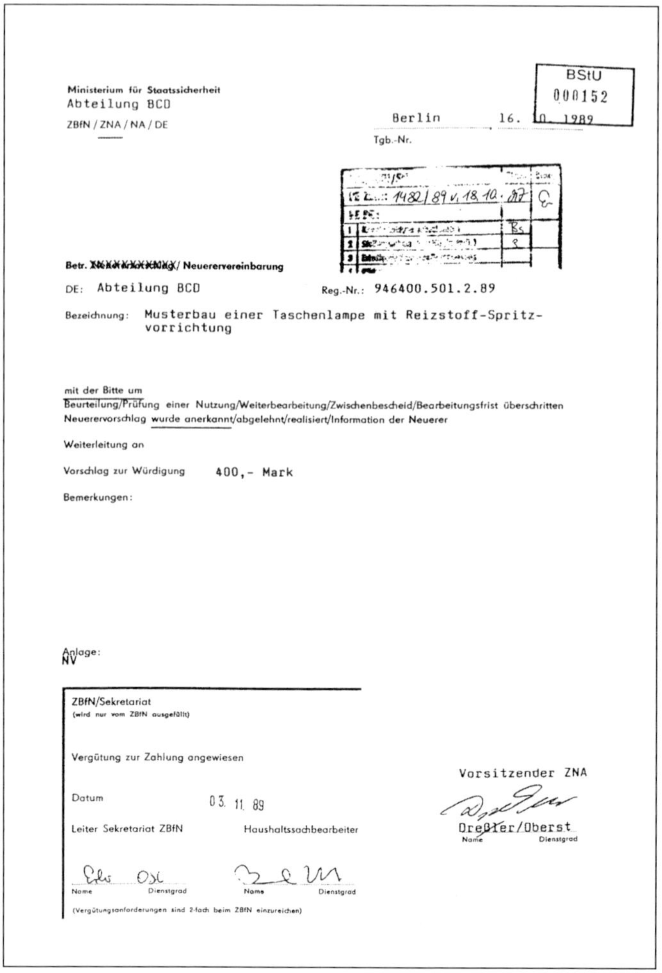

BStU
000152

Ministerium für Staatssicherheit
Abteilung BCD
ZBfN / ZNA / NA / DE

Berlin 16. 10. 1989

Tgb.-Nr.

Betr. XXXXXXXXXXX / Neuerervereinbarung

DE: Abteilung BCD Reg.-Nr.: 946400.501.2.89

Bezeichnung: Musterbau einer Taschenlampe mit Reizstoff-Spritz-vorrichtung

mit der Bitte um
Beurteilung/Prüfung einer Nutzung/Weiterbearbeitung/Zwischenbescheid/Bearbeitungsfrist überschritten
Neuerervorschlag wurde anerkannt/abgelehnt/realisiert/Information der Neuerer

Weiterleitung an

Vorschlag zur Würdigung 400,- Mark

Bemerkungen:

Anlage:
NV

ZBfN/Sekretariat
(wird nur vom ZBfN ausgefüllt)

Vergütung zur Zahlung angewiesen

Datum 03. 11. 89

Leiter Sekretariat ZBfN Haushaltssachbearbeiter

Name Dienstgrad Name Dienstgrad

(Vergütungsanforderungen sind 2-fach beim ZBfN einzureichen)

Vorsitzender ZNA

Dreßler/Oberst
Name Dienstgrad

Confirmation by the Central Office of Enhancement that object was produced by the Armaments Department / Chemical Services Department (November 3, 1989) the former mechanic and former non-commissioned Wehrmacht officer Gotthold Lange. From 1974 to 1988 the qualified metalworker Kurt Voigt served as its director. In its last year the department was directed by the forty-year-old factory metalworker Erich Schwager.

Motor Vehicle Maintenance

The State Security Service was in possession of an expansive fleet of vehicles. Department IV of Motor Vehicle Services was responsible for its maintenance and was also located within the Hohenschönhausen restricted area.

The department was first established in 1974, after Camp X was closed down. Headed by the former deputy camp commander Wilfried Franke, it employed 259 MfS workers in the end. The entire department belonged to the Department of Behind the Lines Services (VRD). The majority of the cars came from the two motor pools of the Main Department of Personal Security (PS) that chauffeured state and party functionaries. It also included the small B 1000 vans, various business cars and busses.

In response to the increase in the number of MfS vehicles, a new 54 meter long and 18 meter wide workshop hall was established in 1982. It stood to the left of the entrance at Genslerstrasse 69–72, right in front of the old Vehicle Repair Shop (KRW). A Guard Regiment (WR) housing unit, a border wall and a watchtower had to be torn down to accommodate it. The one-story hall had various sections serving different functions. The MfS' own technical inspection authority was able to process twenty vehicles every hour. Four cars could be repaired and serviced simultaneously. By 1989 the garage had the capacity to repair 10,000 vehicles per year.

Camp X accommodations building (current view, photo from 2002)

Special Construction

The Special Construction Department (AGM/B) of the State Security Service was also located on the grounds of the Hohenschönhausen restricted area. This department, which belonged to the Ministers Workgroup (AGM), was responsible for building the GDR's important protective structures.

The AGM was the State Security Service's operational center in the case of an emergency mobilization. The 689 employers working under Major General Erich Rümmler in 1989 prepared all the MfS measures to be taken when war or riots broke out. They were responsible for assuring that, as part of the plan to guard against such a threat, one central order would allow for thousands of people to be arrested and sent to camps. In the case of an emergency, citizens of "enemy states," but also politically unreliable GDR residents were to be transported to isolation camps within hours. For a long time AGM was also responsible for the training and deployment of special forces that could engage in attacks, liquidation and sabotage in the Federal Republic of Germany. And finally, the AGM conducted the work of Erich Mielke, Minister of State Security, in the National Defense Council of the GDR.

The AGM/B, which was headed by Lieutenant Colonel Manfred Beulich, looked after the MfS government bunkers and shelters. In the end, its 447 employees managed the necessary forest areas, furnished with firefighting equipment and helicopter landing sites, conducted repair and maintenance work and maintained the facility at a high technical standard.

Communications Department

A section of the MfS Communications Department (N) was also located in the Hohenschönhausen restricted area. It was responsible for GDR State Security Service's internal communications system.

The subdivision N 4 was housed in a building at Freienwalder Strasse 14 and Lieutenant Schulze was the MfS department head in the eighties. The subdivision employed about 120 workers, most of them specialized technical staff, and was responsible for assembling and repairing the cables of the MfS communications network.

Department N was one of the largest offices of the Ministry of State Security. During the popular uprising of June 17, 1953, internal communication broke down in parts because the lines were overloaded. In response, this area was subsequently systematically expanded. Between 1960 and 1989 the staff grew from 67 to 1,559 workers. The former communications mechanic Karl Zukunft has been head of the department since 1964. The division not only organized the communication lines all the way down to the district bureaus and administration offices, but also monitored communication with the SED and state apparatus. It also protected the GDR's secret government networks and diplomatic radio service from infiltration.

Main Department of Personal Security

In the fifties the department responsible for the protection of state and party functionaries was also located in the Berlin-Hohenschönhausen restricted area. Other states usually had a specially trained police force for this purpose, but here too, the SED only entrusted the MfS with this special task. With its 3,762 employees in 1989, the Main Department of Personal Security (PS) was one of the ministry's largest departments. Just how justified the SED was in fearing its own people became especially clear during the popular uprising of June 17, 1953 when protestors throughout the entire country stormed the party headquarters and forced the Politburo to flee to the Soviet sector in Berlin-Karlshorst.

One of the department's main responsibilities was to provide escorts for the leading politicians of the German Democratic Republic and to guarantee their safety during routine travel. By 1960 the department was also responsible for protecting and looking after the needs of the Politburo residential settlement in Wandlitz. It provided the escort commandos during politicians' business trips to other countries and ensured the security of the state and party leadership during public mass rallies on special occasions like the 1st of May. In coordination with the Guard Regiment (WR) in Berlin, it also guarded the SED Central Committee building on Werderscher Markt, the offices of the GDR Minister President and Council of State Chairman, the hospital in Berlin-Buch, the Palace of the Republic and various recreational areas of the politburo members including the Schorfheide hunting grounds. The department also organized the protection of foreign politicians visiting the GDR in cooperation with the security agencies of other states.

The Main Department PS was the second largest department of the MfS. It also supervised the employees of the district administrations and local counties. The department was run by Franz Gold, butcher by trade, until 1974. He was succeeded by his longtime deputy, the technician surveyor Günter Wolf.

The Buildings

The Remand Prison

(map pgs. 6/7: building 1)

The four meter high grey prison walls of the Ministry of State Security's former central remand prison (UHA) at Genslerstrasse 66 can be seen from quite a distance. Watchtowers, reminiscent of the Berlin Wall, stand on the corners. Four different sized buildings are situated behind the strong enclosure: the former canteen with underground cells of the old remand prison, the new three-story building with the prison cell and interrogation wing, the hospital with sick-room cells and treatment stations and the workshop courtyard, where convicted prisoners were forced to work for the MfS.

The Camp

A dark redbrick building, built in the late 1930s by the architect H.C. Bartels, forms the center of the prison compound. Completed in 1939, it was used as a canteen by the National Socialist People's Welfare Organization (NSV).

A unit of the Soviet People's Commissariat of Internal Affairs (NKVD) occupied the building in late May/early June 1945. The buildings were considerably smaller at that time, a fact made apparent by the still-existing façade of the former canteen. Following a brief period of construction, the occupying power established a camp on the grounds that the NKVD designated a "Spezlager", a "special camp." The camp, assigned the number three, was placed – like all Soviet camps in Germany – under the jurisdiction of the Special Camp and Prisons Department, which resided a few buildings away at Genslerstrasse 69–72. This department, directed by the NKVD, was later renamed the Ministry of Internal Affairs (MWD).

In the beginning it was mostly members and low-level functionaries of the NSDAP and its affiliated organizations who were held at Special Camp No. 3. Government employees of different levels were also imprisoned here along with a large number of doctors, press and radio staff, bank employees, artists and actors, including the renowned artist Heinrich George. They were accused of cooperating with the Nazi state and many were brought here on the basis of denunciations and unfounded suspicions. An increasing number of opponents of the Soviet occupation were transported here, among them the Social Democratic party member and commander of the Berlin police force Karl Heinrich, who had previously been incarcerated by the Nazis. He was transferred from the former women's prison

Map of the canteen complex, hand-copied from an original drawing from 1939

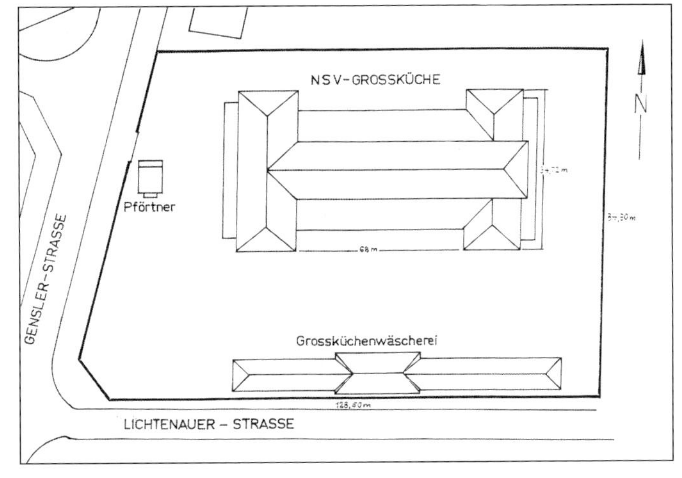

How the Camp was Established

Our work first entailed building a circa 2.5 meter high fence out of boards and pieces of barracks that would enclose an area of about one hectare. We dismantled the cooking cauldron from the canteen and built a temporary latrine about 20 meters long and a few meters wide, a 1.5 meter deep ditch over which the boards were placed lengthways and crossways forming clear rectangles. It was located on the southeast corner of the kitchen structure, about 20 meters away from the building. The permanent latrine was later set up in the southeast corner extension of the building. After this job was completed, I think it was two-story bunks made of boards where the prisoners later slept that were erected in the rooms of the eastern front of the canteen and in the hall of the kitchen. The prisoners used their personal possessions as padding and blankets.

The former prisoner Erich Hermann reports on building Special Camp No.3 in June 1945. *Source: Zeitzeugenarchiv Gedenkstätte Berlin-Hohenschönhausen.*

in Berlin-Lichtenberg to the sick-patient department of the Hohenschönhausen camp where he died on November 4, 1945. By summer 1945, a growing number of young people accused of participating in the National Socialist underground organization "Werewolf" also arrived in the camp. Internment was based on the order issued on April 18, 1945 by Lawrentij Berija, head of the Soviet secret service. It called for the Red Army "hinterland" to be cleansed of saboteurs, spies, terrorists, active members of the Nazi party, members of the police and secret service, government officials, and other "hostile elements" in Germany. For most of the prisoners, the camp in Berlin-Hohenschönhausen was only the first stop of their captivity. They were forced to march from here to the special camps of Sachsenhausen, Ketschendorf, Fünfeichen and Weesow near Berlin. Many of these Soviet camps, such Jamlitz, Sachsenhausen and Buchenwald, were established within former Nazi concentration camps. Between 22,000 and 23,000 prisoners went through the collection and transit camp at Genslerstrasse 22; most of them were German internees from Greater Berlin. According to Soviet records, 886 prisoners died between July 1945 and October 1946. Because of its location within the city, it was difficult to seal off the camp from the outside. And repeated complaints led to its closure in October 1946.

The "U-Boot" ("the Submarine")
(map: building 1)

The empty kitchen building was converted into the Central Remand Prison of the Soviet Ministry of State Security (MGB) in Germany at the end of 1946. Prisoners of the Prison Labour Camp (HAL) in the "Richard Heike" former meat processing machinery factory erected an underground wing with bunker-like cells in the storeroom and cold storage rooms of the former canteen. The underground cell section went into operation in the spring of 1947. The sixty chambers, most of them damp and windowless, were only furnished with a wooden bed and a pail that served as a toilet. A light burned in the cells both day and night. The MGB didn't build in ventilation and partial heating systems until the late forties, but even that didn't change the fact that the

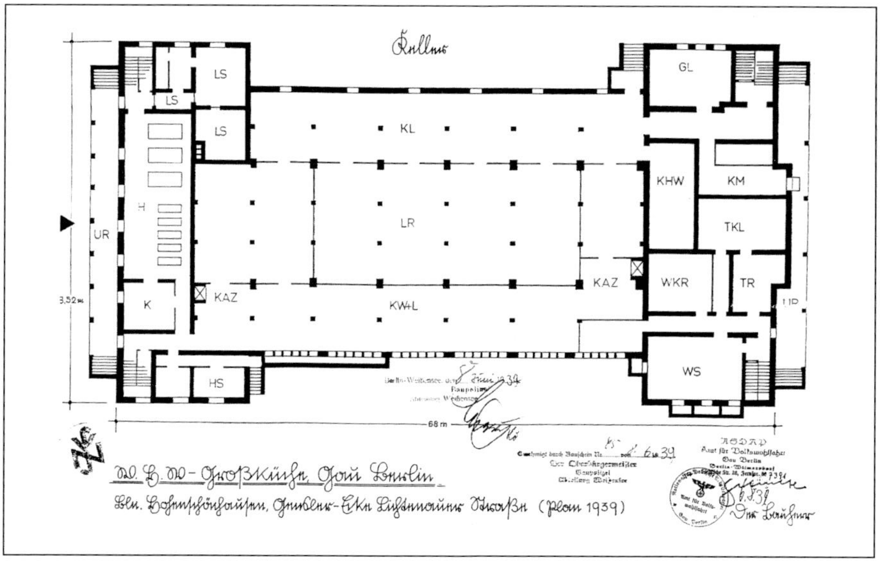

Layout of the basement level of the canteen (June 1939)

prisoners in the dungeon felt like they were aboard a submerged submarine, which is why they called the prison the "U-Boot" ("the submarine"). The hygiene conditions defy description and not only female prisoners found them extremely degrading. To name just one example: until 1951 prisoners were not provided with any personal hygiene supplies such as combs, toilet paper or toothbrushes.

In addition to those suspected of being Nazis, the prison also contained people thought to be political adversaries: members of the democratic political parties including the Socialist SPD, the liberal LDPD and Christian Democrat CDU. But communists and Soviet officers accused of being disloyal to the party were also imprisoned here. The interrogations carried out by Soviet state security officials tended to take place at night and were often accompanied by threats and physical violence. Former prisoners later described how confessions had been extracted from them after they had been deprived of sleep for long periods, had been forced to stand for hours on end, had been kept under close arrest for days or held in water cells. Soviet military tribunals sentenced most of them to many years of forced labour. After the Socialist Unity Party of Germany (SED) dictatorship collapsed, many former prisoners applied for rehabilitation. The Russian authorities have declared almost all of the applicants innocent.

During the "Great Terror" in the second half of the thirties, the Central Committee of the Communist Party of the Soviet Union explicitly permitted the Soviet People's Commissariat of Internal Affairs (NKVD) to use torture methods against "enemies of the people." As a means to break the prisoners' resistance and force them to make the desired statements, the Soviet secret service officers reverted to using these measures in the territory of Germany occupied by the Red Army in 1945. They used "Strafkarzer," a special kind of punishment cell and other cells, erected in all the large remand prisons, to extort confessions.

There is proof that by 1947 a one meter large square standing-only cell existed in the central prison of Berlin-Hohenschönhausen. A low-ceilinged cell existed beneath the cellar steps where prisoners could only squat or sit. There were also chambers with raised thresholds. Inside, buckets of

A prison cell in the "U-Boot" ("the submarine") (photo from 1995)

water were poured on the prisoners for days until the floor of the cell was centimeter high in water.

The torture rooms had no beds, stools, or toilet pails. To intensify the prisoners' suffering, they were only given a small amount of food and drink; sometimes their clothes were removed or they were hand-cuffed or exposed to cold air. Many prisoners lost all sense of time within the chambers; they had hallucinations or suffered a circulatory collapse.

Karl-Heinz Reuter, a former prisoner, reported that he and another prisoner were forced to build special torture contraptions inside four cells in May 1947: a bending apparatus with shackles for hands and feet, kneeling beds and a water-dripping device. His report and sketches provide the only available information about these constructions. In 1993, the Senate Administration for Culture, Science and Research had three cells with torture facilities reconstructed in the "U-Boot" ("the submarine") on the basis of Reuter's description.

The Ministry of State Security took over the basement prison in summer 1951 and used it until 1960/61 as its central remand prison. The conditions under which prisoners were held changed very little under the MfS. Paul Merker, a top SED functionary who had fallen into disfavor and held in Hohenschönhausen from 1952 to 1955, spoke to a cell informer about the regime that was responsible for his imprisonment: "You live here as if you were buried alive, without newspapers and completely cut off from the outside world." The cells, according to Merker, were like stone coffins. Although he was knowledgeable of all the states' institutions, he had not thought it conceivable that such prisons could exist in the GDR.

Threats, physical violence and cleverly devised methods of torture were used in the "U-Boot" ("the submarine") even after the MfS took over. Guidance was provided by Soviet advisors. Systematic sleep deprivation, month-long solitary confinement, standing for hours on end, and many days of close arrest with undernourishment, dreadful degradations and verbal abuse were the common methods used to extract confessions during the fifties. Not until the death of the Soviet dictator Joseph Stalin did Lawrentij Berija, Minister of Interior, order the discontinued "use of arbitrary measures and physical violence" in the remand prisons. Many top functionaries had themselves become victims of the specific methods of torture applied there during the previous years. Now brutally beating prisoners

Basement corridor in the "U-Boot" ("the submarine") (photo from November 1990)

was forbidden. Prisoners could no longer be hand-cuffed for days with their arms twisted behind their back. Long-term sleep deprivation and locking naked prisoners in cold cells was henceforth prohibited. The torture contraptions were to be dismantled.

Prisoners in the "U-Boot" ("the submarine") were no longer to be subjected to systematic violence as a means of procuring a confession, but now and again the interrogators did assault prisoners. Through strict solitary confinement, night interrogations, systematic intimidation and threats of severe punishment, prisoners were put under immense pressure to sign the incriminating interrogation protocols of the State Security Service. These protocols were used as the basis for bringing prisoners to trial and convicting them.

Remand prisoners deemed important by the MfS were held in Berlin-Hohenschönhausen, usually because of what were considered political crimes. The list of prisoners ranges from strike leaders of the 17th of June 1953 uprising to Jehovah's Witnesses. Even reform communists, such as the head of the Aufbau publishing house Walter Janka, and politicians who had fallen into disfavor, such as the former GDR Foreign Minister George Dertinger (CDU), were imprisoned for months in the crypt-like prison. SED critics from the West were even kid-

Conference room in the Central Prison Department administration building. Furniture and chandelier were made by prisoners of a labor commando (photo from November 1990)

napped by the MfS and brought to Hohenschönhausen. The West Berlin attorney Walter Linse, for example, was kidnapped in 1952 and executed the following year in Moscow. Approximately 11,000 people were held in the MfS central remand prison from 1951 to 1989. Most of them came from the GDR, but some came from the Federal Republic of Germany and other countries.

After a new prison was built on the rear grounds, the State Security Service began using the "U-Boot" ("the submarine") in 1961 for storage and sometimes as a work and living area for prisoner labour brigades. The former prisoner kitchen, which could provide up to 250 warm meals, was later used to feed the MfS staff. The MfS had a sauna built for its staff in the former sanitary area of the basement prison in the seventies. In 1966/67, prisoners of the neighboring Camp X added two additional stories to the brick building, which stood over the basement prison. The building served the MfS Prison Department as an office and administrative headquarters. The offices of the Investigation Department were housed on two levels.

The New Prison Building
(map: building 1)

Prisoners of Camp X built an U-shaped, three-story building behind the old prison

Interrogation Methods in the "U-Boot" ("the submarine")

Yes, I was beaten (sporadically). I was beaten with fists. I was hit with a four-cornered steel ruler. During one interrogation I was placed on the table. The head of the Soviet interrogation brigade who sat next to me slapped me on my weak heart with his flat hand in short intervals although he knew that I had already suffered two heart attacks. This torture lasted about two hours. That same night I was kicked in the shin, my head was beaten with fists and my hair was pulled out. At another interrogation that was carried out without witnesses, my glasses were busted. The platinum frame of the glasses was stolen. During other interrogations I was forced to stand for hours. My hands were handcuffed behind my back and I had to face the wall. During the interrogations in 1951 to 1952 I was always handcuffed although there was no way or intention of escaping.

The former KPD (German Communist Party) chairman Fritz Sperling was arrested in January 1951 in the GDR government hospital although he was seriously ill. He was brought to the Berlin-Hohenschönhausen Central Remand Prison (UHA). During a secret trial two years later he was tried as a "war criminal, fascist and agent" and sentenced to seven years in a penitentiary. After he was pardoned in March 1956, a KPD investigation commission declared him innocent. In a letter to the party leadership quoted here he describes in detail the interrogation methods used in the "U-Boot" ("the submarine").
Source: Karl Heinz Jahnke: „... ich bin nie ein Parteifeind gewesen". Der tragische Weg der Kommunisten Fritz und Lydia Sperling. Bern, 1993, pgs. 83/84.

in 1959. In 1961 this replaced the "U-Boot" ("the submarine") as the remand prison. Until early 1990, this building served as the Central Remand Prison (UHA) of the MfS. Passageways connected it to the offices of the prison administration in the older brick building and by 1973 it was also connected to the six-story prefabricated structure occupied by the investigators at Lichtenauer Strasse.

The new prison building was especially designed to meet the needs of the State Security Service: The northern and eastern wings contained a three-story prison cell section with over a hundred one to four man cells. A mezzanine level above it created an attic-like space. The interrogation department was located in the southern wing of the prison building, connected to the cell area by sliding metal gates.

By the late sixties prisoners were delivered by truck to an enclosed area at the northern wing of the prison area. They disembarked after the truck had entered a garage, so that they would not be able to recognize where they were. At the beginning of the cell section there was a gated room with an outer wall of glass bricks. This is where prisoners were forced to disrobe upon arrival. An MfS staff member searched their naked body and all orifices for suspicious objects. Prisoners were registered and photographed in the photo room next to the personal effects chamber. Guard and station supervisor rooms, showers and dark cells existed on all three levels. A medical clinic with x-ray room and dental station was also located in the prison cell wing along with a prisoner store ("Konsum") and a prisoner library. As a special privilege certain goods could be ordered from the store. There were two sound-proof rubber cells and a prisoner kitchen in the basement. Female convicted prisoners who had to work in the prison maintenance had their own prison area. The pump room of the prison building's central heating system and an underground connection to the "U-Boot" ("the submarine") were located further back.

North and west wing of new prison building. The "Rose Courtyard" in foreground (photo from November 1990)

Photo room in the west wing of the new prison building (photo from November 1990)

The cells of the new prison were a considerable improvement over the basement cells of the "U-Boot" ("the submarine"). In the early sixties a cell was furnished with a two meter long and 85-centimeter wide wooden bed with a mattress and blanket. There was a table and stool, both of which were screwed to the floor. There was also a toilet without a seat or cover. There was no window in the traditional sense, or any view to the outside, but a construction of glass bricks and an airshaft did allow for muted light and a little fresh air to enter the cell. Beneath this "window" the heater, which could not be regulated, was covered in perforated metal sheeting. The cell doors,

Rubber cell in the new prison building (photo from December 1991)

Cell in the prison hospital (photo from November 1990)

equipped with a small hatch (the "feeding hole") and a peephole, were covered on the inside by a 1.5 millimeter thick panel of steel. The neon ceiling lights, a control light set into the wall above the cell door and the sockets installed later could only be operated by the guard from the outside. A sink and small double-door wall cabinet for holding soap, a comb, toothbrush, glasses and even dentures were added at a later date. A seat and cover were added to the toilets as well. At the same time the Ministry of State Security had wiretapping devises installed in the cells occupied by multiple prisoners and cameras installed in the corridors. By 1983, the cells, which remained empty during the many months of renovation work, were equipped with warm water and had a mirror set into the wall.

A strict prison regime was enforced in the so-called custody rooms. The standardized rules of conduct for the remand prisoners of the State Security Service and Ministry of Interior were set in the "Joint Instructions on Implementing Detention" of November 8, 1968. Prisoners were particularly unnerved by the fact that their names were replaced by prisoner numbers. When the cell door was opened they were expected to stand in a certain position and identify themselves by number. Many also found it debasing to have guards monitoring them continuously through the peephole, even when they were sleeping or using the toilet. Prisoners were worn down over time by the fact that they were denied human contact for weeks at a time and harassed by a heavily regulated daily regiment even at night. While sleeping, for example, prisoners were not allowed to place their hands under the blanket and their head could not be turned away from the peephole. They were not permitted to use the wooden bed during the day. A special light signal system in the hallways assured that prisoners never saw each other, even when they were being brought to the shower or to the interrogator. The prisoners had no say as to when they took their meals or what kind of food they received. Some had difficulty adjusting to the too high or too low temperatures in the cell. Many prisoners also suffered from the fact that they were denied contact to nature for months and that the guard staff only barked orders at them.

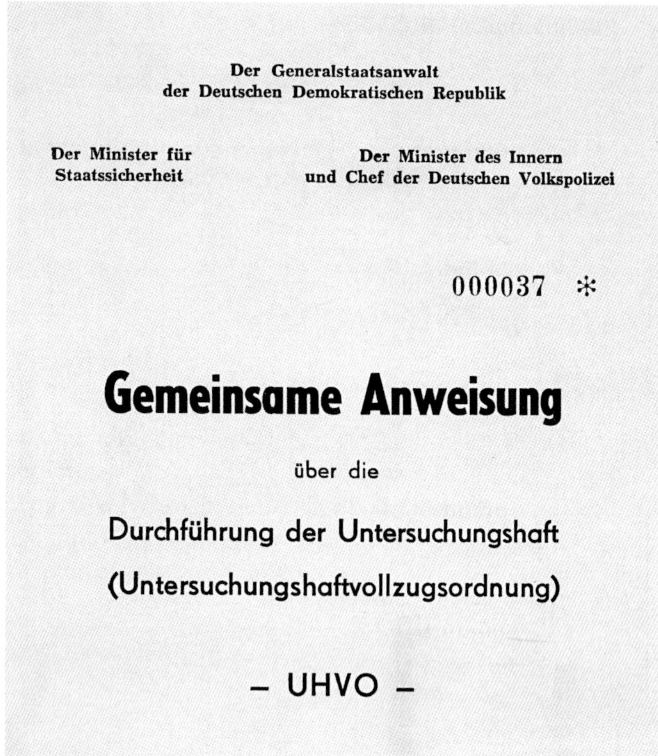
Der Generalstaatsanwalt
der Deutschen Demokratischen Republik

Der Minister für Staatssicherheit

Der Minister des Innern und Chef der Deutschen Volkspolizei

000037 *

Gemeinsame Anweisung

über die

Durchführung der Untersuchungshaft

(Untersuchungshaftvollzugsordnung)

– UHVO –

Joint prison regulations of the Ministry of Interior and Ministry of State Security

Behind the cell wing, on the east side of the compound, there were twelve prison yard cells where the prisoners were locked up outside for up to thirty minutes a day to allow them a bit of fresh air. Each cell, open from above, had a base of four by ten meters and was enclosed by a four meter high wall equipped with an alarm system and barbed wire. Armed guards patrolled the cells from a metal observation bridge. The exercise cells were also monitored by a camera. In the eighties wire netting was added to the cell roofs, leading prisoners to tag them the "tiger cages". Prisoners were brought to the outdoor cells one cell at a

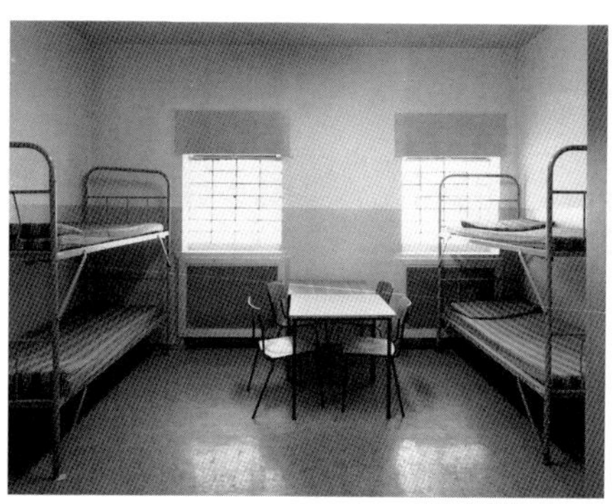

Guards escort a prisoner back to his cell (MfS teaching material, early 1960s)

A four-man cell (photo from November 1990)

Exercise cell in back of new prison building (MfS teaching material, early 1960s)

time and were not allowed to sing or talk during the outing. It was also forbidden to interrupt the exercise break or to come too close to the bordering walls.

The interrogation area in the southern wing of the prison building contained 120 interrogation rooms. The interrogations, often lasting many hours, took place here, sometimes continuing for a period of months. The rooms were furnished with a locked filing cabinet, a desk chair and a desk with a telephone and typewriter. Another cabinet contained the hidden wire-tapping devises. Prisoners usually had to sit on a stool in the corner of the room to prevent them from seeing who entered when the door opened. A prisoner was allowed to take a more comfortable seat near the interrogator when he was signing the protocol or when he was offered a cup of coffee – a

Interrogation room (photo from November 1990)

The Methods of First Lieutenant Hübsch

Hübsch would hit prisoners in a burst of rage about 15 times during three months of detention. "When he got angry," recalled K., "Hübsch would jump up, turn off the tape recorder and plunge toward me." One time he knocked him from the stool with such force that K. rammed his head against the heater. Hübsch kicked him when he was lying on the ground. Norbert K. doesn't remember how he got back to his cell. He woke up next to the toilet with a terrible pain in his leg and hip, his head droned and his ears hurt.

The former MfS interrogator Jörg Hübsch opened an attorney's office with other former interrogators in 1990. In 1999, he was sentenced to six months probation for assault and battery and 6,000 marks in damages for pain and suffering.
Source: Berliner Zeitung from January 15/16, 2000.

special privilege. The interrogator decided whether to close the curtains or whether to leave them open, providing the prisoner with a glimpse of sky not available to him from his cell.

At the beginning of a work session the appointed "investigation leader" entered into one of the interrogation rooms and had the prisoner brought to him. The aim of an interrogation was to bring the prisoner to make incriminating statements that could be used against him in a trial. In some cases, prisoners were physically assaulted.

By the early sixties at the latest, when the Federal Republic of Germany started paying for the release of prisoners, the MfS interrogators began working with methods more refined than the crude brutality of the fifties. They increasingly depended on the scientific research conducted at the MfS Law School in Potsdam-Eiche and taught there as "operative psychology." The interrogators often put pressure on prisoners by threatening them with many years of imprisonment or they had "cell informers" spy on them secretly. They also determined disciplinary punishment and whether or not a prisoner should be granted medical assistance, an outdoor break, visitors, and writing and reading privileges. Like the entire prison regime, the interrogators' activities were aimed towards destabilizing the prisoner and conveying a sense of helplessness to him as a means to breakdown his resistance.

An Interrogator Reports

Use the first minutes of contact to make your adversary so insecure that he'll provide a few starting points upon which you can build up the interrogation. The more statements, passing comments, even behavioral patterns you can make subject of the interrogation, the less you will need to know or reveal about what you don't know.

Adopted from older interrogators and tried out myself on a number of occasions, my tactic aimed at making Ms. L. insecure by conveying the impression that I already knew everything, and that she could only help herself by making forthright statements and that I needed only to clarify a few details in passing so to speak. And continually demonstrate confidence and unlimited power and make it clear to the adversary that he will be treated according to the law, but that he doesn't really have any rights. […]

For example the "good interrogator / bad interrogator" game, that has been used for all times. That should make the accused see "his" interrogator as the lesser evil, in the best-case scenario, as his "confident." The method is relatively simple: Another interrogator – usually a supervisor – participates briefly in the interrogation, attacks the accused, acts cynical, threatens – "no more Mr. Nice Guy!" –, yells and then leaves the room. The actual interrogator, who stayed in the background the whole time, on occasion using gestures and facial expressions to convey how unpleasant he finds all this, only reappears then. "Now that my boss is back outside we'll manage with each other, won't we?!"

Uwe Karlstedt worked in the eighties as an interrogator in Berlin-Hohenschönhausen and was in Main Department IX, responsible for prosecuting "political underground activities."
Source: Regina Kaiser / Uwe Karlstedt: Zwölf heisst „Ich liebe Dich". Der Stasi-Offizier und die Dissidentin. Cologne, 2003, p. 53.

Central Prison Hospital

(map: building 2)

The MfS Central Prison Hospital (HKH) was located on the south side of the prison complex until 1990. The original one-story building, completed in 1939, first housed the laundry room, two apartments and the garages of the neighboring National Socialist People's Welfare Organization (NVS) canteen. Towards the end of the forties the interrogation rooms and administration of the Soviet remand prison were located here.

In the fifties the Ministry of State Security expanded the building and converted it into a medical station. By 1960 it had become the HKH. It was founded as an independent department, but by 1974 it was being run by the MfS Central Medical Service (ZMD).

Prisoners from the MfS' seventeen remand prisons were treated in the prison hospital both as in-patients (Department 2) and out-patients (Department 1). The hospital doctors also provided psychological expert opinions for the public prosecutors and courts. The HKH did not recognize the principle of medical confidentiality. Medical evaluations and personal statements made by prisoners were communicated to the Main Department IX to assist the investigative work. The MfS doctors did not act as the patients' counselors, but were instead part of the system of political persecution.

The prison hospital contained prison cells with 28 beds for female and male patients. There was also an x-ray ward, a morgue, laboratories and various treatment and operating rooms (including gynecology, dentistry and physical therapy). Three more exercise cells were added to the east section of the building during the final expansion in 1972.

Dr. Wolfgang Dorr was the first director of the prison hospital in 1960/61. He was followed in 1962 by Dr. Richard Uhlig and in 1964 by Dr. Harald Haarfeld. The medic Bernhard Landes became head of the department in early 1969. Dr. Herbert Vogel took over the directorship in the mid-eighties and oversaw 28 employees in 1989.

The workshop courtyard: work and lodging area for the men's labor commando (photo from November 1990)

Workshop Courtyard

(map: building 3)

A workshop courtyard for convicted prisoners had existed on the north side of the prison compound since the early sixties. It contained a few workshops, a number of garages and, in the early years, a small nursery with greenhouses. A small unit of male prison inmates had to perform various work for Department XIV here and in the former "U-Boot" ("the submarine"). Approximately 25 metalworkers, electricians, carpenters, plumbers, masons and painters were put to work repairing company vehicles, building furniture, doing maintenance work and renovations. They also cared for the heating system in the basement of the brick building and fed it with coals.

The labour unit was first housed at the back of the old canteen on the first floor. The greenhouses were dismantled when the enclosed area for trucks delivering new prisoners was erected in the new prison building. The inmates were no longer permitted to use the underground passageway between the "U-Boot" ("the submarine") and the new building, which is why the prison administration set up new lodgings for the male labour unit in the workshop courtyard.

The Memorial

The Berlin-Hohenschönhausen Memorial on the grounds of the former remand prison is a product of the peaceful revolution in East Germany: If the citizens of the GDR had not gone out onto the streets in the fall of 1989 and demanded free elections, the grounds would probably still function today as a remand prison of the Ministry of State Security.

After the closure of the prison in October 1990 the Berlin Justice Administration planned to convert the building for 2.5 million marks into a penitentiary for day-parole prisoners. However protests from prisoners and civil rights activists led to other considerations. In July 1991 the administration resolution to permanently close down the prison was carried out. Three months later the Berlin Senate recommended "the erection of a dignified memorial on the grounds that facilitates a suitable commemoration of the victims' suffering while allowing the inhumane cells in the so-called 'U-Boot' ['the submarine'] to be preserved for public viewing." The Berlin Parliament passed a similar resolution in 1992. That same year the prison building was placed under protection as a historical monument.

After standing empty for a time, the building was opened in June 1994 for scheduled viewings, made possible with help from a job-creation program. The Berlin-Hohenschönhausen Memorial was founded in December 1995. At the same time scholars were preparing a concept for the future use of the grounds. In June 2000 the Berlin Parliament passed a law to erect a memorial site as an independent foundation under public law. Its aim is to "research the history of the Hohenschönhausen prison from 1945 to 1989, to provide information through exhibitions, special events and publications, and to encourage a critical awareness of the forms and consequences of political persecution and repression under the communist dictatorship."

The former prison is visited by more than 200,000 people each year, including approximately 110,000 schoolchildren and trainees. During a tour of the grounds – usually led by a former inmate – visitors are shown the basement where the canteen and underground cells had been and the new prison building built by the Ministry of State Security. The outdoor exercise cells of the prison hospital are also part of the tour. For security and structural reasons, important areas of the prison, such as the former sick-room cells, the lodgings of the labour units, and the sauna for the guard staff can only be shown in exceptional cases. A permanent exhibition is going to be presented in the hall of the former canteen.

Investigative Offices

(map: building 4)

The expansive work area of the MfS investigators surrounded the remand prison like a clamp. Since the seventies the Main Department IX, which operated as the so-called investigative organ of the GDR Ministry of State Security, was located right behind and adjacent to the prison. The six-story prefabricated structure on Lichtenauer Strasse and the office building behind it still exist today.

By the sixties the investigators had already begun complaining to the MfS headquarters about an acute lack of space. The continually expanding main department

Staff of Investigation Department on Lichtenauer Strasse (March 1988)

lacked a conference room for the leadership, and a recreational and common area for personnel summoned to Berlin from other districts. A staff room for superior officers and for a planned evaluation and control group (AKG) was also needed.

The MfS provided the funds and material needed to cover plans for the five years from 1971 to 1976. They planned to erect a new building behind the prison, but before construction could begin the area had to be separated from the grounds of Camp X. The building material storage and processing grounds that had been located there since the sixties was removed.

The leadership of the main department was able to move into its new headquarters on Lichtenauer Strasse in 1973. The prefabricated structure, labeled House 50 B, provided about 160 workspaces and various other rooms. A passageway connected it to the interrogation wing of the prison. A wiretapping center that monitored all of the interrogation rooms was set up in the basement.

The MfS building company "Spezialhochbau" (special structural engineering operations of Berlin) added a three-story "module" in 1978. This office building, which stood vertical to Lichtenauer Strasse was also connected to the main building by a passageway. It contained an additional 65 offices as well as two meeting and storage rooms for the MfS investigators.

Single and semi-detached middle-class houses (No. 2–32) used to stand on the south side of Lichtenauer Strasse. They were built in the 1930s and inhabited mostly by skilled workers, public servants, salaried personnel and retired persons. By the summer/fall of 1945 the Soviet occupying power evacuated the houses – along with other only temporarily occupied privately-owned property on Gensler and Lössauer Strasse and on Arendsweg – so that they could be incorporated into the secret service zone. They were then occupied by officers of the neighboring Special Camp No. 3, the "small" Prison Labour Camp (HAL) on Freienwalder Strasse. Staff of the Special Camps and Prisons Department moved in here since the beginning of 1950.

Around 1952, after the State Security Service took over the complex, mid-level MfS personnel lived in the buildings on Lichtenauer Strasse and at Genslerstrasse 63 a. They lived close to their offices, which were located in the restricted area. Hans

Bialas, director of the remand prison, lived with his family at Lichtenauer Strasse 18. In 1953/54 Hans Mühlner, who was transferred to Prison Department XIV and promoted a year and a half later to head of Department XVI (prison surveillance), lived at Genslerstrasse 63 a.

In 1976 the Ministry of State Security decided to tear down the buildings at Lichtenauer Strasse 2–32 because they were rundown and no longer suitable as housing. By then only a few were still being used by the State Security Service as a dormitory for young MfS staff. The buildings, garages and fruit trees were removed in spring 1977 and a parking lot with ninety parking spaces for MfS staff was created in their place. A motor vehicle hall was added around 1979. Staff of the Main Department IX parked "court exhibit" automobiles here and examined them for criminal evidence. These were the cars that the MfS had confiscated from people, such as escape helpers, who had been arrested. The building provided space for 25 vehicles and had additional storage areas. A security wall was eventually erected on a five meter wide strip facing Lössauer Strasse so that the area could be fenced off, hidden from view and sound-proofed. By 1976 Main Department IX had another garage complex built to the east of the prefabricated structure on the former Camp X grounds to provide more space for confiscated vehicles and directors' company cars.

The residential building on Genslerstrasse 63a was still in good condition and therefore spared demolition in spring 1977. By 1976 it was used as the facility headquarters of the restricted area. This branch of Main Department IX was created on August 7, 1975 on the basis of directive no.

An Investigator on his Way to Work

I pass by the vehicle barrier, controlled by soldiers of the guard regiment, the troop I was enlisted to, but never joined.
I can already see the prison grounds in front of me and head in that direction. To my right stands a building complex. I have learned through whispered rumors that the forgery workshops of the MfS are on the inside. I pass by the gated old building with its barred windows and decorative Wilhelminian style façade. This is where the Main Department IX/II is situated, the department that deals with locating Nazi and war criminals who are still alive. Behind it lies the archive, where the reference and court files were kept before they were moved to the headquarters in Lichtenberg in the late eighties. Next door stands the large building of the "Operative and Technical Sector" (OTS), which contains a number of laboratories and where I have been a few times to pick up expert opinion reports such as script analyses.
Finally, I arrive in front of the tall prison walls with the sliding steel gate. There is a small door next to the gate – one could almost miss it. An observation slit at eye level. I show my ID for the second time, this time to staff of Department XIV, which is responsible for prison security. I go around the U-shaped prison building and side wing where the interrogation offices are located and arrive at the Main Department IX administration building.

Source: Regina Kaiser/Uwe Karlstedt: Zwölf heisst „Ich liebe Dich". Der Stasi-Offizier und die Dissidentin. Cologne, 2003, pgs. 92/93.

20/75 issued by Minister Erich Mielke. In cooperation with the forces of the Guard Regiment (WR) it had the responsibility of physically screening off the restricted area from the outside. It also had the task of implementing the health, work, and fire prevention regulations.

The facility headquarters regulated and controlled the entire pedestrian and vehicle traffic in and out of the restricted area. It registered all non-MfS employees who entered the restricted area. The commander could arrest anyone suspected of endangering the security of the restricted area at any time and "initiate all measures necessary to clarify the circumstances." The office was also responsible for making sure the outer security installations functioned properly.

The facility headquarters consisted of the commander, his deputy and the person on duty at the main gate reception office on Freienwalder Strasse. Captain Rüdiger was facility commander until 1978 after which Major Jochen Pfeffer took over.

In 1990, after the investigative department was closed down, the former office complex of Main Department IX initially came under the authority of the GDR Ministry of Interior. After that it briefly housed the State Office of Criminal Investigation of the new (former East German) federal states. In the late nineties the garage of confiscated vehicles and other facilities on Lichtenauer Strasse including the in the meantime fire-damaged facility headquarters office were torn down. Nineteen semi-detached family homes were built on these grounds in 1998.

Parking lot of Prison Department and Investigation Department hall of confiscated vehicles (March 1988)

Labour Camp X

(map: building 5)

The grounds of the GDR State Security Service former motor vehicle maintenance service was located at Genslerstrasse 69–72, right next to today's memorial site. The 7,535 square meter terrain originally belonged to Richard Heike's meat processing machinery factory. In 1921 the owner built an assembly hall and a four-story office building attached to a flat storage facility. The production and storage rooms built on the neighboring property (formally Genslerstrasse 68) in 1919 and 1922 also belonged to Richard Heike.

Over the years the buildings were leased to various companies and sometimes redesigned or expanded by the new users to suit their needs. By the end of the war the "Erwin Neuendorf. Häute und Felle. Import-Export" (Erwin Neuendorf's Animal hides and Furs Import-Export Company) had its headquarters at Genslerstrasse 69–72. It was the only company in Berlin with a wholesale permit to buy and sell dry furs. In the spring of 1945 the production department of the Asid Serum Institute and the Asid Press Plant was located at Genslerstrasse 68, but the company's buildings had suffered severe war damage.

The grounds at Genslerstrasse 69–72 were briefly occupied by the Red Army and in early July 1945, it was used to accommodate the Special Camp Administration Department of the Soviet People's Commissariat of Internal Affairs (NKVD)/Ministry of Internal Affairs (MWD). Because of the important role that the Asid Company played in providing medical supplies for Greater Berlin, it was permitted to continue working there for a time. The company produced vaccines and serums to control epidemics and the Allied occupying forces imposed strict conditions on its continued production. But the Soviet secret service regarded the production site as a security risk because of its close proximity to the secret Special Camp No. 3. Under pressure from the MWD, the Serum Institute and Press Plant were forced to give up their location at Genslerstrasse 68 in June/July 1946. The Special Camp Administration Department took over the buildings.

The Special Camp Administration Department was a central instrument of Soviet repression in Germany. It was based on directives no. 00315 and no. 00461 of the Soviet People's Commissariat of Internal Affairs of the USSR that were issued on April 18 and May 10, 1945 by Lawrentij Berija, calling for the establishment of special camps. The department, formed from the camp administration of the 1st White Russian Front under Marschall Schukow, first had its headquarters in Fürstenwalde. It was first in charge of eight, later ten special camps and a number of large prisons run by the NKVD and MWD in the Soviet zone of occupation (SBZ). According to Soviet information from 1990, 122,971 Germans were interned in the camps; more than a third, 42,889, lost their lives there.

In May 1949 the department consisted of twenty officers, forty guard troop members and an unknown number of drivers. They were divided into leadership, secretariat, political apparatus and guard units, and were responsible for six work areas that were broken down further into subdivisions: surveillance, regime and identification, operative activities, cadre, finances, economy and first aid. The department heads were Colonel Michail E. Swiridow (May 1945 to June 1947), N. T. Zikljajew (June 1947 to April 1949) and Wladimir P. Sokolow (April 9, 1949 to March 1950).

The special camps were first under the authority of Berija's deputy, Colonel General Iwan A. Serow. After he returned to Moscow and a major prisoner release campaign was carried out in early spring 1948, a number of camps were closed. The remaining inmates were concentrated in the Bautzen, Buchenwald and Sachsenhausen camps. The Special Camp Administration Department thus lost its independence and was demoted to one of 22 subdivisions of the Main Administration of MWD Camps (Gulag).

The complex at Genslerstrasse 68–72, referred to internally as the "town," consisted of three large structures. The department staff offices and various storerooms were located in the Erwin Neuendorf Company's four-story office building and the connecting flat-roofed building on Bahnhofstrasse. The large hall was used as a car garage. The barracks of the guard commandos, a dining room, a club, numerous prison rooms, the main guard headquarters and a supplies and food storeroom were all located in the former main building of the Asid Serum Institute. The grounds were protected by a meter and a half high boarded fence. To prevent an attempted assault on the department, machine guns were positioned at three points on the north and east side.

After the last Soviet camps in the GDR were closed, the Special Camp Administration Department was also liquidated in April 1950. That same month the Soviet Ministry of State Security (MGB) representative in Germany, General Major Grigorij A. Melnikow, received over 160,000 registration cards from Colonel W. P. Sokolow with the recorded releases of German and foreign inmates.

In 1951 the Ministry of State Security took over the completely run-down grounds. A small group of prisoners, masons, electricians and metalworkers from the Waldheim penitentiary were forced to erect a prison labour camp on the grounds where the Soviet remand prison had stood. The former Erwin Neuendorf Company warehouse was renovated and converted into a Vehicle Repair Shop (KRW). Within nine weeks the forced labourers had enclosed the grounds with a three meter high wall reinforced by barbed wire and four massive watchtowers. The labour camp was ready for use by December 1952.

The Camp X or Commando X – as it was referred to internally by the MfS – was the GDR State Security Service's only penal institution. People convicted of political and criminal offices by the Soviet Military Tribunal and the East German courts were imprisoned here. A few Nazi criminals such as Paul Sakowski, the "hangman" from Sachsenhausen, were also held here. By the late fifties the majority of inmates incarcerated here were criminals, including quite a few dangerous ones. According to current estimates approximately 8,000 prisoners came through the camp.

The prisoners worked in the motor vehicle garage, in repair and special workshops, in the laundry room, construction offices and on building sites. They serviced the vehicles of the GDR government and the State Security Service. They also designed and erected additional MfS remand prisons and office buildings. They built residential buildings and facilities for the MfS athletics association "Dynamo," including the ski jump in Klingenthal and the Sport Forum facility in Berlin-Hohenschönhausen.

The prisoners' daily routine was modeled after the Soviet forced labour camp. There was a "prisoner self-administration" within the camp, which meant that prisons appointed to special functions were responsi-

View of Camp X from Bahnhofstrasse (mid-1950s)

Forced Labour for the MfS

To ensure that the workshops of the H.A. Administration and Economy in Freienwalder Strasse are working to their full potential, it will be permitted for members of the SfS [State Secretary for State Security] to submit limited work requests – mainly repair work – when there are otherwise insufficient contracts to maintain full operations.
The work contract will be issued by the responsible staff member of the HA. [Main Department] of Administration and Economy, Construction and Property.
Members of Department XIV are not authorized to issue jobs from staff.
The invoice for staff members should be based on the amount of time employed in accordance with the customary negotiated wages for the labour group in question (carpenter, upholsterer, etc.). Any a dditional costs for material must also be calculated. The amount of payment due is to be deducted from the salary by the finance department on the basis of HA. Administration and Economy accounting.
Preferential treatment for orders should be given to comrades who themselves were subject to penal labour as prisoners [refers to former Nazi prisoners].

Memo excerpt from Ernst Wollweber, State Secretary for State Security, on June 26, 1954 to the head of the main departments and independent departments in the State Secretariat for State Security.
Source: BStU, MfS VRD 56, Bl. 7.

ble for a large part of the internal organization. By the second half of the fifties, a sophisticated informer system was in place causing widespread mistrust among the prisoners. Every inmate had to consider carefully what he confided to whom since there was also the risk of denunciation. Prisoners reported making insubordinate comments or violating rules could be punished with many days of close arrest in a penal cell.

It was view of the State Security Service that sentencing convicted prisoners to a camp was not only punishment, but also a means to educate them socially and influence them politically. The camp leadership therefore encouraged the inmates to engage in cultural and athletic activities. Competitions, film showings, television, political agitation, cultural evenings and professional training were a part of camp life. Camp X, as a reformatory to improve the inmates, reflected the GDR as a whole, since its population was also exposed to constant surveillance and communist indoctrination.

The camp's existence was kept strictly secret during the era of the GDR. To keep it concealed, the – limited – prisoner mail was sent to other prisons, first to Luckau, later to Berlin-Rummelsburg. And the inmates were also transported to these locations when they received visits from family. They were not allowed to speak with anybody about their actual whereabouts and activities.

Responsibility for Camp X was shared by different divisions in the fifties: Surveillance and organization was in the hands of the central Prison Department XIV. The prisoners' work deployment, however, was organized by the Main Department of Administration and Economy. From 1960 to 1974 the camp was subordinate to the newly formed Department XVI, which was respon-

Sketch of Camp X by Herbert Richter, prisoner in the Camp (second half of the 1960s)

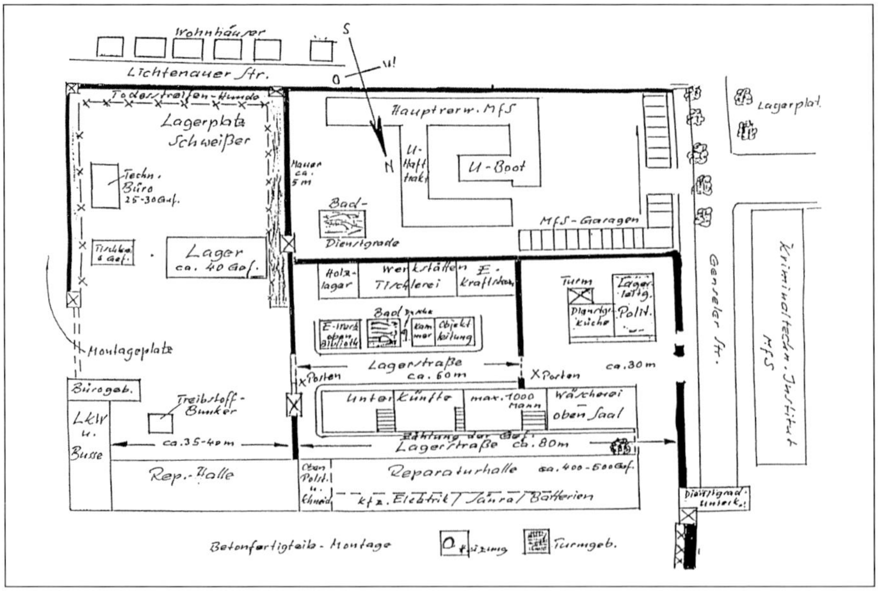

sible for the surveillance of all MfS prison institutions. Prisoners' activities were henceforth planned and controlled by the Main Administration B (acquisitions). Police counselor Karl Keilhofer was the first camp leader (1952/54), followed by Captain Ludwig Hartmann (1954–1959). The labour camp was later commanded by Lieutenant Colonel Paul Rumpelt (1960/1961), Major Kurt Zimmermann (1961–1964), Lieutenant Colonel Günther Zabel (1964–1968) and Lieutenant Colonel Hans Mühlner (1968–1974).

The prisoners were first housed in a two-story section of a building previously belonging to the Asid Company (House C 2 today). During the first few months they had to build a massive fire extinguisher water basin (between House D and House F) and a flat-roofed building for the workshops (House E today). They were also supposed to repair the Erwin Neuendorf Company's high-rise office building for MfS personnel which no longer exists today. The 9.5 x 25 meter large water basin was equipped with a diving tower and starting blocks so that the inmates could use it as a swimming pool. Today the basin serves as a parking lot, but the starting blocks and the lettering on the swim lanes are still clearly visible.

The building where the prisoners were housed was rebuilt and expanded in 1953/54 and an extension was added to the gabled wall. In the back section (House C 1 today) the camp administration set up a depot and later additional prisoner quarters. A laundry room was located on the ground floor of the wing facing Genslerstrasse (House C 3 today) with a two-story high hall above it. In the laundry room inmates cleaned and ironed textiles from the camp and remand prison along with the clothing and uniforms of the MfS staff, the Berlin Guard Regiment (WR) and "Dynamo" athletics association. The prisoners took their lunch and spent their free time in the hall that houses a canteen today. They performed – usually monthly – theater and musical productions as well as other entertainment here.

A massive barrack was erected on the site of the volleyball court in front of the fire extinguisher water basin (House D today). It contained a clothes storage room, an HO store, an upholstery workshop, shoemaker, and the Camp X prisoner self-administration. The main entrance to the camp contained a sliding steel gate. In the second half of the fifties the camp leadership had its headquarters moved to the right of the entrance gate, requiring prisoners to enlarge the former guard house, converting it into an administration building (House B 1 today). In addition to the offices on the first floor, the main guard house, and the staff kitchen with dining room on the ground floor, there were about ten detention cells in the basement used to punish camp inmates. The camp administration's business vehicles were parked in the garage (House B 2 today) along the wall to the interrogation prison. The entire MfS work area, which prisoners could only enter when summoned, was separated from the camp grounds by a wall and a gigantic electronically-operated metal sliding gate. The external wall facing Genslerstrasse has since been torn down but the inner wall still exists.

At the same time that these structures were being built an additional extension was erected behind the fire extinguisher water basin (House F today). Due to its location prisoners referred to it as the "lakeside building." The ground floor initially contained a depot distribution station for building and tool equipment. A commercial and engineering office was located on the first floor.

In the early sixties the warehouse was expanded as part of the plan for "new area expansion." Mason brigades had to erect two L-shaped saw-tooth roofed halls (House K today) to the east of the old Vehicle Repair Shop (KRW). In 1963/64 a bodyworks area with a paint shop was established here

Fire extinguisher basin in Camp X (photo from March 1996)

MfS Staff Member's Notes

Comrade Major Sachse in House III of Department XIV is employed as operative staff.
He fulfills this responsible task to the complete satisfaction of his supervisors. He works completely independently.
Comrade Major Sachse understands how to acquire and direct his own factors, thus making it possible to promptly recognize escape attempts and break up hostile prisoner groupings. He plays an active leadership role in the base organization and has an instructional influence on the comrades. Based on his positive achievements which have been important part of ensuring the security of our building and to provide an incentive for even better work, we propose awarding Comrade Major Sachse a financial bonus of 400 DM on the occasion of the anniversary of the German Democratic Republic.

Proposal from Hans Bialas, head of Department XIV, from September 12, 1958 to provide a bonus to Major Otto Sachse, head of operative work in Camp X. *Source: BStU, MfS KS 162/63, Bl. 42.*

with a repairs section for trucks and busses. The old plant was connected to the new production site by a building bridge on the first floor.

Camp X was closed down in June 1974. Following an amnesty granted to political and criminal offenders, the number of prisoners in the camp fell considerably. The camp grounds were also reduced in size to accommodate other construction plans.

Department IV of Motor Vehicle Services took over complete control of the maintenance and repair of the ministry's own vehicle fleet and government vehicles at Genslerstrasse 69–72. Like the supplies service, which continued to run the dining hall and laundry room, it belonged to the MfS Department of Behind the Line Services (VRD). This department was formed from Main Department of Administration and Economy and the Main Administration B (acquisitions).

In the early 1990s the GDR government gave the buildings at Genslerstrasse 69–72 to the state-owned Autoservice Berlin (today called CSB Car Service Berlin GmbH). After reunification the NBL real estate company of Berlin purchased the property from the trust agency. In the early nineties the new owners removed the outer wall with the sliding gate that had served as the entrance area to the camp. They also tore down a 1980s building that stood parallel to Genslerstrasse. In 1996 the KRW hall that was built in 1921, the four-story "high-rise" and the single level multifunctional building from 1982 on Genslerstrasse were all dismantled. A car dealership with exhibition floor, carwash, body shop and parking deck was erected in 1997 at the site of the former repair garage. A section of the fire extinguisher water basin was broken off in March 1998 to create more parking spaces. Meanwhile an industrial area specializing in automobile repair and service has established itself at Genslerstrasse 69–72.

The "Graveyard"

There used to be a "graveyard" from Special Camp No. 3 situated behind the tracks of the Tegel-Friedrichsfelde industrial railway at Gärtnerstrasse 19–26. The bodies of dead prisoners were buried here in mass graves on a four by five acre plot of land. The NKVD chose to use the former Wehrmacht map depot grounds as a gravesite because it contained so many bomb craters and shell holes. In July/August 1945 the prisoner burial commando hastily buried the first camp dead, most of whom died of a gastrointestinal disease epidemic.

The dead were sometimes "buried" so close to the surface that heavy rainfall was enough to re-expose the corpses. Residents of Berlin-Hohenschönhausen, who searched the grounds for useful materials during the day or who used the trail between the train station and Gartenstrasse, became aware of the buried bodies.

Complaints from residents and fear of an epidemic led the Weissensee police station to make a request in 1945 to the camp commander Captain Tschumatschenko to rebury the estimated 200 to 250 bodies. Instead of responding, the captain blocked off all access to the "graveyard," posted military guards at the entrances and had a fence erected about ten meters from Gärtnerstrasse 19–26. He commented to the German office that it was enough "to shovel sand or earth over the corpses and have them stay put." Henceforth the deceased of the special camp were buried in two meter deep and two and a half by four meter large mass graves. They were presumably strewn with carbide sludge that had been disposed of in the former fodder silos located on the grounds.

The carbide, a residue left behind by industrial gas manufacturing, was an important building material in the highly deficient postwar era and led to a conflict between

Corpses on the Dump Site

On 8.8.45 around 4.30 pm Frau Elisabeth Lollek, Bln.-Hohenschönhausen, residing at Berliner Strasse 140, appeared and reported that a corpse lay buried on the debris dumping grounds in Bln.-Hohenschönhausen, Gärtnerstrasse. The investigation thus far found 37 corpses there. The corpses have only been there for a few days. The Criminal Investigation Bureau will continue to investigate.

Excerpt from a work report of police precinct 287, Berlin-Hohenschönhausen from August 9, 1945. *Source: LAB, Rep 148/1, Nr. 147.*

the Weissensee building office and the camp administration. The building office repeatedly tried to acquire the sludge accumulation on Gärtnerstrasse. In late October / early November 1945 the district commander Colonel Atajew agreed to make the material available without seeking approval from the camp administration that had prohibited entrance to the grounds. The attempt by the building office in Berlin-Hohenschönhausen to follow up on the granted permission and remove the carbide from the silos ended in a fiasco. A camp guard prevented the transport and arrested one of the workers – Herbert Berg, resident of Grosse-Leege-Strasse 62. Because the administrations in Weissensee and Hohenschönhausen did not take any apparent action to have the single father of two children released, his brother Bruno made an appeal to Dr. Arthur Werner, the Head Mayor of Berlin, on November 12. The major immediately instructed the District Mayor of Weissensee, Max Knappe, to "contact the responsible local commander in order to achieve the release of Herbert Berg." The next day the problem was discussed and negotiated with Colonel Atajew. The district commander now qualified his original agreement, explaining that the carbide in Hohenschönhausen that was located within or near the fence could clearly not be mined "because the guards on duty will of course shoot." He intended to "conduct an investigation" regarding the whereabouts of the worker. Whether this was ever done is not known.

Health Authorities Report

The following was subsequently ascertained about the discovered corpses: The grounds on Gärtnerstrasse are located close to a concentration camp run by the Russian occupying forces. The inmates who died in this camp are buried at night in the shell holes of the 4–5 acre open area. A number of other shell holes filled with corpses were found. An exact number cannot be given. This situation cannot continue since the danger of an epidemic increases with each day. A report to the district administration and the Health Authority for the Removal of Grievances has been sent. An effort will be made to find a gravesite where the bodies can be immediately reburied.

Excerpt from a summary report by the Weissensee police department from August 20, 1945 on the corpses found on Gärtnerstrasse. *Source: LAB, Rep. 148/1, Nr. 147.*

Temporary memorial plaque at the Berlin-Hohenschönhausen cemetery (photo from 1995)

Until today it could not be ascertained what happened to Herbert Berg. It is known that a second request was made by the district office that also remained ineffectual.

Between June 1945 and October 1946, 886 dead from the special camp and the Soviet prison labour camp on Freienwalder Strasse were buried at the "graveyard." Other deceased persons from the Prison Labour Camp (HAL) and probably from the Hohenschönhausen and Berlin-Lichtenberg remand prisons continued to be buried there until 1948. How many is not known.

The district command headquarters demanded that the grounds remain off-limits. Signs in both German and Russian announced that trespassing is prohibited. It appears that the property, which was officially under the trust administration of the Weissensee property office since 1950, was not released by the Soviet occupying power for another year.

During the following period the state-owned Berlin landscaping company, the VEB Grünanlagenbau Berlin, maintained a storage area on the grounds. Up through the sixties meter-high heaps of building debris were piled up over the mass graves. After that the parking lot of a plate production plant run by the state-owned building agency in Berlin, the VEB Wohnungsbaukombinat, was located on the grounds of the "graveyard." In the early nineties the "FATEC Fahrzeug und Baumaschinen Vermietungs-Service GmbH" (vehicle and building machinery rental service company) took over the property.

In 1995 witnesses helped to locate the exact location of the mass grave. The bones of 127 dead were recovered beneath a thirty centimeter thick concrete surface and debris filling that was at times 2.6 meters thick. The remains were buried at the Hohenschönhausen old town cemetery at Rhinstrasse, located at the corner of Gärtnerstrasse, on October 24, 1995. An ecumenical funeral service was held and attended by the mayor of Berlin Eberhard Diepgen. The bones of 122 other inmates found during excavations were buried at the same site on December 15, 1999.

In 1998 a so-called memorial area designed by Manfred Höhne was dedicated on the cemetery grounds. The designer's father had died in the Special Camp No. 3. The centerpiece of the memorial is the "DenkSteinFeld", a field of stones containing approximately one hundred tons of stones gathered from around Berlin. Strewn across a 1,300 square meter meadow, the different sized stones symbolize the mostly anonymous dead of the Soviet prison. Their "disorder" aims to show how difficult it is to establish clear categories of victim, accomplice and perpetrator among the dead. Visitors can walk through the field of stones and may even add or turn over stones. The area is enclosed by a thorny hedge, which

Warning sign in two languages near the "graveyard" on Gärtnerstrasse (1953)

runs along the palisade walls and the labyrinth-like entrance and symbolically embodies the pain and hopelessness of the prisoners. Schoolchildren from the 4th Special Education Support Center in Berlin-Lichtenberg have taken over the responsibility of looking after the memorial. Each year on October 24 a ceremony to commemorate the dead is held at the cemetery.

The Factory

(map: buildings 6–9)

The production site of the Richard Heike meat processing machinery factory had stood for many years at the corner of Freienwalder Strasse 17–19 and Grosse-Leege-Strasse 95–96 a. The factory building has by now been mostly torn down and a supermarket stands on the site today.

Two large iron-truss halls formed the center of the old factory facility, which was built by the architect R. Lots in 1910/11. Richard Heike, the company owner, had the two halls connected by three cross buildings in the 1920s. He also built another industrial building, with two levels in some parts, at Grosse-Leege-Strasse 95–96. It was positioned next to the hall and had a courtyard behind it.

By the summer of 1945 the industrial factory had just begun with its "peacetime production" when it was occupied by the Soviet People's Commissariat of Internal Affairs (NKVD) and integrated into the prohibited zone that was being established. Major General Aleksej M. Sidnew, head of the NKVD apparatus in Berlin, ordered that a prison labour camp consisting of "combined workshops" be set up for the repair of "every kind of motor, automobile, electric, gas and radio device, clocks, clothing, footwear and more." The workers were drawn from the population of prisoners in the Soviet special camps in the Soviet zone of occupation (SBZ).

The labour camp was used by the Berlin Operative Department as a kind of skilled crafts enterprise. The prisoners took care of repair and construction work for the Soviet secret police free of charge. In the camp's vehicle workshop, prisoners were forced to give a makeover to stolen luxury limousines and equip them with high-capacity radios with multiple amplifying levels. The camp building brigade was also responsible for converting the former canteen into the Central Remand Prison of the Soviet state security service in the Soviet zone of occupation (SBZ). From the end of 1946 to the spring of 1947 about 75 prisoners were in-

View of the "Heike Factory" with administration building on Freienwalder Strasse 17–19 (ca. 1912)

Soviet Car Thieves

I am employed as a chauffeur for the Free Labour Union of Berlin, in Berlin C, Wallstr. 63/65. On Saturday evening, August 8, 1945, around 5:30 p.m., I had just completed my tour and parked my car in the garage at Bln.-Hohenschönhausen, Berliner Str. 89.
Another car, an Audi, not yet ready for use, was parked in the same garage. The driver of this car arrived at my apartment around 10 at night and informed me that my car had been stolen by members of the Russian occupying troops. My colleague's car was also hauled off by the Russians with a truck no. T 74 819. His car was an Adler model no. G 1–934. I knew that the Russian soldiers who work at the Heike Company drive the car model T 74 819. So I went directly to the commander and was appointed two officers to accompany me. We went to the Heike Company where we had to wait out front while the accompanying Russian officers went into the plant. While we were waiting outside the building, I suddenly saw my car driving along Goeckestrasse toward Heike. We ran right to it, the car stopped, and we questioned the passengers, a Russian officer and a Russian in civilian clothing, and demanded that they return my car to me. The officer was halfway ready to give my car back to me but the civilian Russian resolutely refused. After talking for a long time, both officers invited us to take a seat in the car.
Since we didn't know what the two of them were planning to do with us, we refused and went back to the Heike Company to get help from the two officers. Meanwhile the two Russians drove off with my car.

Excerpt from a report of police precinct 287, Schöneicher Strasse 3–4, about a car stolen by officers of the prisoner camp on August 20, 1945. *Source: LAB, Rep. 148/1, Nr. 147.*

Entrance area of restricted area with the former "Heike Factory" (mid-1950s)

volved in building an underground wing of cells and various interrogation rooms inside the building. The also carried out masonry work in the nearby Soviet restricted area at Lake Obersee and Lake Orankesee, and in the Lichtenberg, Pankow and Prenzlauer Berg prisons.

The prison labour camp served high-level NKVD functionaries as a way for them to increase their personal wealth. Illegally acquired booty and trophies were collected here, repaired or altered when necessary and then sent to the Soviet Union. "Radiolen," which are radio-gramophone music boxes that radio specialists had equipped with up to six loudspeakers, were particularly coveted by the Soviet generals. The former head of the Soviet secret police in Berlin, Major General Sidnew, was even arrested in 1948 as a consequence of these kinds of personal gains.

Preliminary estimates suggest that about 1,500 interned forced labourers came through the Soviet Prison Labour Camp (HAL) in Berlin-Hohenschönhausen. The camp was closed down at the end of 1948 and the remaining inmates were sent to Buchenwald und Sachsenhausen.

At first, when the MfS took over the restricted area, it used only a few of the Heike plant buildings. A motor vehicle camp was established in the 74 meter long and 30 meter wide iron-truss hall that ran lengthwise on Grosse-Leege-Strasse. The main entrance to the secret service zone with a guard house and registration area was located at the end of this hall, at Freienwalder Strasse 19. The street was first blocked by a simple barrier, but by the eighties a two meter sheet-iron gate cut right through the street.

Beginning in 1958 the entire factory complex went through a number of stages of re-

A "Marauder" as Head of the Secret Service

The Soviet secret police in Berlin was headed by Aleksej Matwejewitsch Sidnew during the first postwar years. Born in 1907, he became a professional soldier at the age of 21. After joining the Communist Party, he was trained as a military engineer. By summer 1941 he served duty at the front in a special unit of the NKVD. In 1944 he became deputy head of counterintelligence of the 1st Ukrainian Front and a year later was called back to the NKVD by Serow.

Ranked as a major general, Sidnew served as head of the NKVD/MWD/MGB in Greater Berlin from June 1945 to December 8, 1947. In this position he was in charge not only of the Berlin operative sector, but also of the Central Remand Prison and the small prison labour camp in Hohenschönhausen.

At the end of 1947 Sidnew was appointed Minister of State Security in Tatar SSR in Kasan. His rapid advancement was followed by an equally rapid fall. Sidnew was accused of embezzling a hundred sacks filled with more than eighty million Reich marks from the assets of the Berlin Reich Bank after the war. In his defense he claimed that it had been agreed upon with the deputy NKVD chief Serow that the money would go towards fina ncing operative activities.

During the investigation six hundred pieces of silver cutlery, about a hundred pieces of platinum and gold jewelry, and 17th and 18th century French tapestries were also found in his apartment in Leningrad. Sidnew was consequently arrested for embezzlement on January 28, 1958 and committed to a psychiatric clinic for involuntary treatment in October 1951.

furbishing, conversion and expansion. The Main Department of Administration and Economy set up a printing press in the two-story industrial building and courtyard on Grosse-Leege-Strasse that was taken over by the Department of Behind the Lines Services (VRD). It functioned as Department IV for the Supply Service (VD) and had 35 employees in the end. The Printing Press Department was divided into three subdivisions and directed by Lieutenant Colonel Eberhard Holstein. Printed material for the State Security Service – brochures, identification papers, certificates, envelopes, forms and notepaper – was printed here using book and offset printing methods. The printing press was furnished with modern machinery and could produce both small and large printing jobs. There was a bookbinding shop and copying office connected to it.

Special Building Operations of the "Ministers Workgroup" (AGM/B) that was created in 1961 moved into other areas of the old factory. The employment unit in charge of erecting and maintaining protective structures took over the flat-roofed building next to the printing press, the extension added to the northern gable of the motor vehicle hall and the former blacksmith's shop erected in 1910 at Grosse-Leege-Strasse 96 a.

Storage hall of Department of Behind the Lines Services (1974)

The Main Department of Administration and Economy set up another material and spare parts storage area for the automobile repair service inside the iron-truss hall. The MfS had only taken the most necessary of measures to secure the building structure due to financial constraints. The motor vehicle service took over the building grounds in 1974. Another camp area located in front of the printing press and spare parts camp at the corner of Freienwalder Strasse 19 and Grosse-Leege-Strasse 95 was converted into a parking lot for MfS staff in 1985.

The hall, which stood directly behind the administration building of the Heike factory, was completely rebuilt by the Ministry of State Security. Storage rooms and office space were set up over two stories and occupied by the MfS Central Archive, which contained kilometer long shelves of files and millions of personal registration cards. When the department moved its headquarters to Normannenstrasse in Berlin-Lichtenberg, the space was again redesigned.

Between 1985 and 1987 the State Security Service central weapons and radiology workshops were housed here. Sections of the special tasks unit of Armaments Department/Chemical Services Department (BCD), responsible for weapon and munitions engineering, also moved here. When the GDR State Security Service was dissolved in 1990 the Suhl Vehicle and Hunting Weapons Plant took charge of liquidating this area.

In the nineties the trust sold the plant grounds and the Heike factory administration building to the Lidl Services Company. The chain company opened a discount supermarket in the building at Grosse-Leege-Strasse 96a – a new structure that the MfS had built in the eighties at the site of the old blacksmith's building. The other storage buildings and workshops on the grounds were demolished. The guard house on Freienwalder Strasse 19, which had once served as the central entrance to the restricted area, was destroyed by arson and later torn down. In summer 2003 the ruins of the historic iron-truss factory hall that had also been damaged by fire were dismantled after the hall was removed from the Berlin list of historical monuments to be preserved. That same year Lidl had a new supermarket and parking lot erected on a section of the newly leveled grounds.

Nazi Archive

(map: building 10)

The building at Freienwalder Strasse 17 with its ambitious and decorative façade is a pleasant change from the rather mundane structures of the State Security Service. It is the so-called "Heike-Villa," built by the businessman Richard Heike in 1911 as a residential and administrative building. The prestigious character and simple art nouveau elements can still be seen today on the four-story building designed by the architect R. Lots. The ground floor contained exhibition rooms for German and foreign customers of the meat processing machinery factory. There was a registration and post office, a commercial and engineering office, workspaces for correspondents and an authorized signatory on the first floor as well as various rooms for the company boss. The second floor contained an archive, a dining hall and a conference room. The Heike family lived on the third floor and a laundry wash and drying room was located in the attic.

After the Soviet troops occupied the Hohenschönhausen industrial area, the villa became part of the restricted area. Little is known about how the villa was specifically used in the first postwar years. According to witnesses, interrogation leaders of the Soviet Ministry of State Security (MGB) were also active here.

After the State Security Service took over the restricted area, the head of the Main Department of Personal Security (PS) lived in the "Heike-Villa" for a short time in 1951. An antenna was placed on the roof of the building. The radio communication office set up on the top floor maintained contact with the escort vehicles of government and party leaders. By the early sixties the State Security Central Archives set up its leadership headquarters here.

In 1968 a unit moved into the building that would also prove important to West Germany's political development: the Nazi Archives of the MfS. Immediately following the war, disguised employees of the Communist Party of Germany (KPD) began collecting and preserving countless Nazi files that were then transferred to the MfS in the early fifties. Nazi documents from the political police (K 5) and numerous German files transported to the Soviet Union did not end up in official archives but instead landed with State Security Service. The files were used to check the past of functionaries and to exert pressure on potential informers. By 1956 the MfS had ousted the police from involvement in pre-trial investigations of Nazi murder crimes.

In the sixties documents from the period of National Socialism acquired new importance once the Socialist Unity Party of Germany (SED) increasingly understood how to use them as an effective propaganda weapon against the Federal Republic of Germany. In a well-planned campaign against leading politicians in Bonn including Hans Globke, State Secretary in the German federal chancellery office, and West German President Heinrich Lübke, the MfS conveyed the impression that old Nazis were sitting in most positions of power in the West German government. The MfS engaged in elaborate research to find incriminating documents, supported them with their own personally-created documents and distributed them at

MfS Nazi Archive (current view, photo from 2002)

international press conferences, in brochures and through sympathizers and journalists in the Federal Republic of Germany. In the early sixties the SED and MfS staged a propagandistic show trial against certain implicated politicians such as Theodor Oberländer, Minister of Expelled Persons, and State Secretary Hans Globke. The suspected persons were sentenced in absentia to long prison sentences.

By 1963 the MfS acquired Nazi material on more than 100,000 people and systematically increased its collection over the following years. In May 1964 the GDR Council of Ministers resolved to establish a special "document center," in which all the documents from the period of the Hitler dictatorship that had yet to be evaluated would be compiled. Over 360 people spent months combing through the archives collecting incriminating material against leading members of the West German federal government as well as high-level members of the Bundeswehr (West German Army), police and judiciary. The most important documents were completely or temporarily confiscated by the MfS.

The MfS established an independent work unit in 1965 to compile, append and examine the documents. In December 1967 Erich Mielke gave the order for the establishment of a new department at Freienwalder Strasse 17. The documents from the Nazi era were to be systematically procured and utilized "for engaging in targeted exposure of people active in the state, economy and military apparatus, in parties and organizations in West Germany and [...] West Berlin who are encumbered by their fascist past." The Main Department IX/11, headed by Lieutenant Colonel Lothar Stolze, officially began its work on February 1, 1968 and put together a huge Nazi archive by examining more and more newly attained files. The archive was not accessible to outsiders, but the State Security Service staff could help themselves to information whenever they chose to.

The Main Department IX/11 also provided assistance in criminal investigations of murders committed during the Nazi period. Starting in 1960, Department IX conducted pre-trial investigations on 113 convicted "Nazi and war criminals." Following a decision made by the SED leadership, the department also processed requests for legal assistance from other countries and supported the activities of foreign memorials such as the Holocaust Memorial. Whether and when proceedings were initiated or whether a foreign institution received assistance always depended on political and intelligence considerations. For example, the German Democratic Republic chose not to pass on its investigation findings on the whereabouts of Nazi perpetrators like the presumed murderer of the KPD chairman Ernst Thälmann because it wanted to be able to accuse the West German judiciary of not pursuing these matters. There was another case of a doctor from Jena who was believed to have participated in the euthanasia crimes committed by the Nazis. The MfS chose not to initiate proceedings against her because she had meanwhile risen to the position of professor in the GDR and had been distinguished as a "merited doctor of the people."

In the eighties the Nazi Archive at Freienwalder Strasse was given additional responsibilities in other areas: to research the communist resistance against the Nazi regime and – as part of the MfS interest in fostering tradition – to analyze the intelligence apparatus of the KPD and its work with the Soviet secret service. By 1989 the department, which had been headed by Lieutenant Colonel Dieter Skiba since August and which employed about fifty people, had examined 9,000 meters of original documents. Its index card files on individuals contained 1.3 million entries.

On February 8, 1990, after the State Security Service was closed down, the Central GDR National Archives took over the Nazi Archive and its specialized library containing 7,000 books. A branch of the archive with twelve stack rooms, 36 work rooms and various archive installations was set up at Freienwalder Strasse 17 – designated House 3 by the MfS. Effective on October 3, 1990 and in accordance with Article 13 of the unification treaty, responsibility for the Nazi Archive was handed over to the German Federal Archives. Its holdings were moved to the Potsdam department with a branch in Berlin. By May 1992 the Federal Archives had transferred the files from the Freienwalder Strasse to an intermediate archive in Berlin-Hoppegarten. The "Heike-Villa" was converted into temporary refugee housing for asylum-seekers who had fled the civil war in Bosnia. In the early nineties the building was added to the Berlin list of structures to be protected as historical monuments. It has remained empty for many years and is falling into disrepair.

Laboratories and Workshops

(map: building 14)

The main entrance to the expansive grounds of the Operative Technical Sector (OTS) had been located across from the "Heike-Villa" at Freienwalder Strasse 12. A guard house and barrier still exist there today. The complex included other buildings at Genslerstrasse 13–14 and at Werneuchener Strasse 19a. Some of the buildings (Genslerstrasse 13, Freienwalder Strasse 12a) had already been integrated into the restricted area in 1945 and were used by the Soviet state security service as a storage and garage area.

After 1951 the Central Register and Archives Department of the MfS was housed on the grounds. The State Security Service operated a small prison labour camp at the end of 1952 inside the administrative building (House 6) and the production and workshop wing of the former mirror factory on Freienwalder Strasse 12a that no long exists today. The secret prison bore the

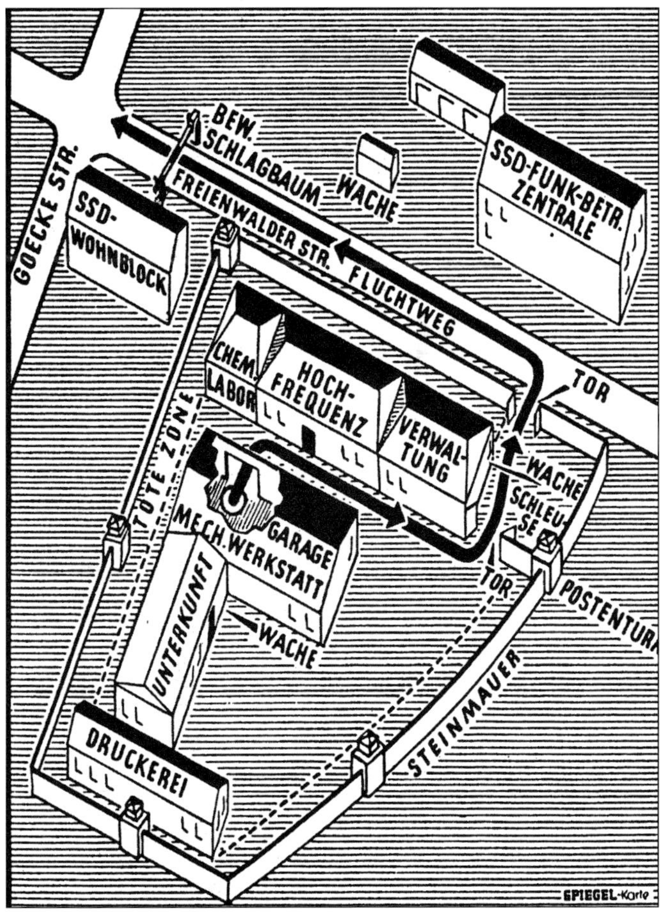

Map of Special Camp X with route taken by two prisoners who escaped in July 1954 (1954)

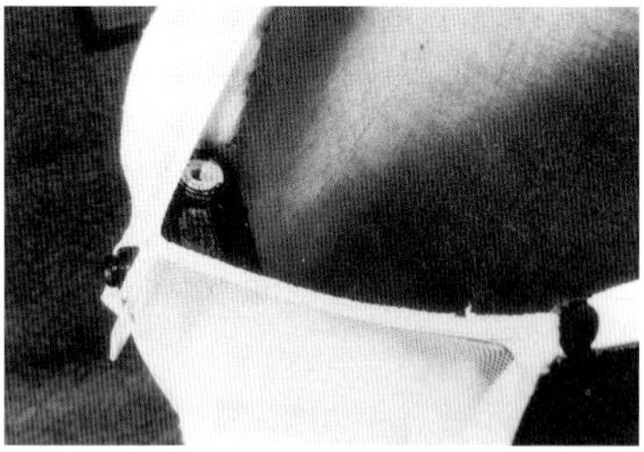
Espionage camera hidden in a bra, produced by the State Security Service

code name "Planning Site S" and was called Special Camp X by the prisoners.

The planning site was responsible for bugging telephones and apartments and for eavesdropping on conversations. Approximately 75 prisoners from GDR penitentiaries – scholars, engineers, and communication technicians – were forced to develop and produce various espionage implements in the camp. This included special tape recorders, wiretapping devices, key-copying sets disguised as matchboxes, miniature cameras in cigarette lighters, mechanisms to quickly change car license plates and devices to inconspicuously open letters. The camp contained a series of modern specialized workshops for fine mechanics and optics, radio and electric technology, printing and automobile mechanics. There was also a machinery hall, a tool-making workshop and various experimentation rooms. The camp administration was located in the office building of the former mirror factory, which it shared with the high-frequency department and the chemical laboratory. The prisoners had living quarters there and their own kitchen. The entire complex was secured by a high wall, watchtowers and a massive iron gate.

The camp was initially part of Department S, later known as Main Department S (operative technology), commanded by Major Rudolf Weber. After the area of operative technology was restructured and the Main Department was dismantled, its administration was taken over by Department K (development of operative-technical means) headed by Lieutenant Colonel Herbert Pörs in 1955. The Special Camp X was closed in 1956 – probably because it had been uncovered and numerous incriminating articles had appeared in the Western press.

Fake License Plates

I said that I had been commissioned by Department S to build tracking device casings and had to order tracking instruments from the radio technology plant in Oberschöneweide where these parts are produced. I also disclosed that West Berlin license plates were produced for business measures carried out by Department S and that the Department possessed a photograph of an original stamp from the West Berlin chief of police that was made from a West Berlin license plate. Stamps were produced using this photograph and the necessary West Berlin license plates were made. I also revealed that in the Department S workshop trucks were built to look like prisoner transport vehicles. They have built-in tracking receivers to detect radio signals. These vehicles are disguised to look like HO or private bakery delivery trucks. Department S gets the car bodies and motors from the "Phenomenon" company in Saxony.

Excerpt from a confession made by Johannes Schmidt during his period of remand in the MfS prison in 1955. The former employee of the State Security Service had reported in West Berlin on his activities in the Main Department S.
Source: BStU, MfS GH 187/79, Bd. 1, Bl. 13.

Little is known about the work of the Operative Technical Sector (OTS) that was set up in 1960. What activities took place in which building at what time can seldom be deduced from the documents that have been examined until now. Only rudimentary information is available about the building activities of the OTS in the restricted area of Berlin-Hohenschönhausen.

The head of the OTS probably resided in the seven-story prefabricated building at Genslerstrasse 13. This is where the Josef Berthoty wire netting factory building originally stood, which became part of the Soviet prison camp in the summer of 1945. In the sixties Main Department IX parked the confiscated vehicles of imprisoned people here. After the building was torn down, the green seven-story prefabricated building was built in 1972/73 with space for 260 workers. The building that was praised for its "high level of technical equipment" also housed a branch of the Central Medical Service and its hygiene inspection unit. The branch was directed by a department doctor and also contained a physiotherapy center.

The expansion of the surveillance state of the GDR also led to the extension of the OTS complex in Hohenschönhausen: In 1980 the Building Department of the State Security Service erected a 74 meter long and 24 meter wide storage hall at Werneuchener Strasse 19a. In 1985/86 three more functional buildings were added. A square four-story building with production and office rooms (House 22) was erected behind the prefabricated building at Genslerstrasse 13 and connected to the front building by a ground level passageway. A flat-roofed building lying vertical to the street at Genslerstrasse 14 is believed to have contained the garages and staff rooms of OTS drivers. The hall behind it (originally House 26) was also used by the OTS as storage.

Production and office building of the Operative Technical Sector on Genslerstrasse (current view, photo from 2002)

The building construction continued beyond the end of the State Security Service: construction of two laboratory and office buildings with a water-treatment facility at the site of the former mirror factory at Freienwalder Strasse 12a (House 12 and 14) had begun in 1989 and was completed a year later. The MfS and its successor organization had meanwhile ceased to exist.

In January 1990 the "state-owned enterprise for scientific appliance construction" took over the OTS complex in the former restricted area. The enterprise, which was soon renamed WIGEBA GmbH, was subordinate to the Ministry of Science and Technology in the GDR. Hundreds of former MfS members who had previously developed espionage, wire-tapping and security technology now joined its staff. After re-unification WIGEBA stopped its operations. Today a business association, a vocational school for cosmetics, engineering offices, small industrial companies and a few doctors' offices and shops reside on the former OTS grounds.

Forensic Institute

(map: building 14)

Diagonally across from the former Genslerstrasse prison gate stood a long two-part building complex. One half ran parallel to Freienwalder, the other half to Genslerstrasse. The building framework was erected by prisoners of the Camp X in 1962. The

The forensic institute on Genslerstrasse, with garages of prison workshop courtyard in front (photo from November 1990)

two three-story buildings which are connected by a stairwell were built on empty grounds that the business man Richard Heike had used for gardening. Berlin handicraft companies were also involved in the interior work of the laboratories and offices.

In 1963 the leadership of the Operative Technical Sector (OTS) moved its offices into the building section at Freienwalder Strasse 16. The sector was primarily responsible for developing and manufacturing surveillance technology. The same year its ancillary Forensic Institute (KTI) moved into the wing on Genslerstrasse. Later the OTS Department 32 (natural science expertise) and 34 (chemical and photographic agents) emerged from the institute. The leadership of Armaments Department/Chemical Services Department (BCD) probably moved into the building section on Freienwalder Strasse in the early seventies.

Armaments Department/Chemical Services Department and Forensic Institute (current view, photo from 2002)

After the German Democratic Republic collapsed, the Department of Nature Conservation and Parks and the Building Surveyors Office of the district of Berlin-Hohenschönhausen moved in temporarily. A motor vehicle repair service has used the garages since 1998. At the same time an electronics recycling business set up its offices on the ground floor wing on Genslerstrasse.

On the Bahnhofstrasse

The street sign at the end of Genslerstrasse still indicates that the Berlin-Hohenschönhausen freight depot train station once stood close to the prison grounds. Prison transports left here for penal camps in the Soviet Union in the late forties.

At the time a first-aid station and lodgings for officers from the Soviet special camps were housed in the reddish-brown factory building at Bahnhofstrasse 7–9. The two-story brick building with an office wing was built by the businessman Richard Heike in 1923 and used by various companies until early fall 1945. The Udylite Corporation for Rust Protection, which produced erosion resistant casing from galvanized cadmium and nickel was the last business to work here. After that the Special Camp Administration Department confiscated the building and made it part of the Soviet restricted area.

The Ministry of State Security took over the complex, but chose not to use the factory grounds. Only the expansive courtyard area remained part of the secret service zone. In 1981/82 the Department of Behind the Lines Services had an entrance and exit driveway built south of the brick building for the Motor Vehicle Maintenance department at Genslerstrasse 69–72. A new guard tower and parking lot were also erected at the eastern building gable. The "Berlin Socialist Wholesale Business for Sports Articles and Cultural Goods," which was located at Freienwalder Strasse 28, maintained a warehouse inside the factory building.

The brick building was placed on the Berlin list of historically protected buildings in 1995. Car Service Berlin GmbH turned it into a temporary sales hall for used and commercial vehicles in the late nineties.

View of the athletic equipment storage area on Bahnhofstrasse, where the rust protection company existed until 1945. Driveway to Motor Vehicle Services area in foreground (March 1988)

Chauffeur Offices

The factory and property owner Ludwig Winterberg ran an enamel and sheet-metal plant at Schöneicher Strasse 8–10 in the twenties. When this ceased to be profitable, he closed down the production site and converted the space into small apartments and business rooms in 1953.

A garage complex emerged on the courtyard grounds with space for about fifty passenger vehicles and delivery trucks as well as a gas station with a Shell double gas pump. About twenty of the garages survived the war.

Between February and August 1947 the Soviet secret service confiscated the property at Schöneicher Strasse 8–10 in a number of different stages. The residents were evicted from the building along with the Alte & Co. perfumery, a sports articles manufacturer, a car repair service and a coal lighter factory.

After the restricted area was handed over to the GDR State Security Service, the chauffeur service of the Main Department of Personal Security was located in the garage complex. It included a permanent on-call staff of drivers and the main government vehicles of the type BMW, Skoda, Tatra and SiS. In 1958 the MfS ceded the smaller building sections on Schöneicher Strasse 8–10 to the neighboring Weissensee retail cooperative. At some point in the late fifties or early sixties the State Security Service gave up the entire grounds. A state-owned taxi service was established on the grounds.

There was no commercial activity on the property in the first half of the nineties. The planned demolition of the garage complex had yet to occur as this text went to press because the building company hired to do the job filed bankruptcy.

The office building at Schöneicher Strasse 9–10, built in the twenties and redesigned in 1931–35 by the architect Erich Gerlach, was placed on the Berlin list of historical monuments on April 4, 1996.

Office of Main Department of Personal Security on Schöneicher Strasse (photo from 2002)

Guard Commando

(map: building 13)

The red brick building at Freienwalder Strasse 16, which is surrounded by the former MfS Forensic Institute and an emergency power facility that was erected in the sixties, was built in 1915/16 as a warehouse based on a design by the Berlin architect Richard Opitz. Later the owner Richard Heike rented it to various industrial enterprises, the last of which was the "Deutsche Syrolith-Fabrik Arno Breitkopf" (Arno Breitkopf German Syrolith Factory), which produced artificial horn and yarn.

In July 1945 the Soviet troops occupied the building for a short time and dismantled some of the equipment inside. In March 1946 the company received orders from the labour camp commander to evacuate its production facilities within three days. The Soviet Ministry for State Security set up its headquarters in the factory. It seems to have functioned as a command center for the entire restricted area of Hohenschönhausen and may have also been responsible for the one at Lake Obersee and Lake Orankesee.

After the GDR State Security Service took it over, a guard unit of the Main Department of Personal Security moved into the building in the fifties. In the early seventies the Department BCD occupied rooms in the front building wing. Around the same time the Hohenschönhausen Special Commando of the guard division established its staff rooms in the back area of the building. When the printing press expanded, it was forced to relinquish its older rooms on the second floor of the industrial building on Grosse-Leege-Strasse 95–96 and in a front building of the large factory hall on Freienwalder Strasse.

Telephone Center

(map: building 12)

An inconspicuous building cased in sheet metal and displaying only a few windows on the upper levels stands on the corner where Freienwalder Strasse merges with Genslerstrasse, right across from the former prison gate.

Communications Department (current view, photo from 2002)

Until spring 1946 the grounds were used for storage by the Coal Separating Limited Liability Company, which conducted experiments with pulverized coal for the Wehrmacht during the Second World War. It later became a part of the Soviet prison labour camp. In the fifties a building material and coal stockyard existed on the grounds and used the former loading station and factory track connection to the former industrial railway. At least until 1964/65 there were still animal stalls here with about ten pigs, which were fed leftovers from the kitchens in the restricted area.

In 1975 the Ministry of State Security erected the two-story hall structure that was used by the Communications Department. Subdivision 4, responsible for the communication networks of the State Security Service, presumably operated a telephone switchboard here for the MfS units in the Hohenschönhausen district. Internally the building was known as the "GWN Headquarters." Plans in the nineties to have the Ministry of Interior use the facility were not realized.

Data Processing Center
(map: building 15)

Computer Center of Main Department A (current view, photo from 2002)

The cube-shaped building at Genslerstrasse 15 with the "Allbüro" sign housed the electronic computer center of the State Security Service during the era of the GDR.

The grounds were first run by the Reiser limited partnership, which produced machinery for street construction. It was nationalized in 1972 and incorporated into the state-owned Street Maintenance Company. The MfS purchased the grounds in the late seventies and had a two-story structure built there.

Internally known as "Object A," the building was equipped with special technology. It had centrifugal pumps, small cooling towers and various climate control units, including steam humidifiers. The interior was handled as a special security zone and the entire facility was protected by a two meter high wall.

The MfS central data processing center moved into the new building in July 1980. Designated Department XIII, it was responsible for all questions relating to electronic data processing. It was not only in charge of the data processing center, but also developed software projects for other departments and provided the MfS with the necessary computer technology. Officially, the department, which had been headed by Lieutenant Colonel Gunnar Hartling since 1976, was subordinate to the Central Evaluation and Information Group (ZAIG). The computer specialists most likely left Hohenschönhausen in 1983/84 to join the other 449 staff members at the main headquarters in the Wuhlheide in the Berlin district of Köpenick.

"Object A" at Genslerstrasse 15 consequently took charge of the espionage apparatus of the Main Department for Reconnaissance (HV A) that used it for similar purposes. The workgroup "Electronic Data Processing" (AG EDV) moved into the building and was promoted to HV A-Department XX in 1988, which was last headed by Lieutenant Colonel Peter Feuchtenberger. The electronic data processing center in Hohenschönhausen was headed by the unit's deputy director, Major Michael Arndt.

The workgroup focused on applying the use of data processing equipment and communication technology to foreign reconnaissance work. This entailed infiltrating foreign networks and databanks as well as other forms of computer espionage. In the late sixties the workgroup began to save the information in electronic databases – until then information had been put on index cards – so that it could be used for computer-supported research. The oft-discussed SIRA storage system (System for Information Research of the MfS Main Department A) was developed here and used to reveal which agent had delivered which report at what time. The system, which consisted of many different partial databanks, served HV A as a research aid but also allowed it to evaluate its sources and derive statistical information. Unlike so many of the documents of HV A, the electronic data was spared the order from GDR government to be destroyed. Years later the data was decoded by an employee of the Federal Commission for the Records of the Stasi and is today an important aid in researching espionage conducted by the MfS on the West.

The building was first used by the GDR computer combine "Robotron" in 1990 and later briefly by the "Allbüro" company.

"Gorge Box"

(map: building 16)

A large canteen at Genslerstrasse 17 looked after the physical well-being of the MfS staff in the restricted area. Before the State Security Service took it over in the late seventies, the area was used by various building companies for storage.

The two-story "dining facility" which opened on January 19, 1981 covered an area of 64 by 41 meters. Headed by First Lieutenant Heinz Danz, it was run by the Supply Service division of the Administration for Behind the Lines Services. Due to the irregular work shifts at the MfS – interrogations often took place at night – the canteen was open on weekdays from six in the morning until one o'clock at night. There was seating for over 400 staff members working in the restricted area. Secret service officers were served by regular soldiers in the "directors' dining hall" and on special occasions, such as business meals with the delegates of brotherhood associations.

The canteen closed down in 1990. Different companies moved into the building briefly in the first half of the nineties. The building has been empty since then.

Canteen (current view, photo from 2002)

The "Town"

During the GDR era there were a number of residential buildings in the area around intersection of Freienwalder Strasse and Grosse-Leege-Strasse which were used by the staff of the State Security Service. The buildings directly across from the main entrance of the restricted area were also part of the secret service zone for a short time.

On March 27, 1947, thirteen apartments in the four-story tenement building of 1910 at Freienwalder Strasse 20 were evacuated on orders of the Soviet commander headquarters in Weissensee. It can be no coincidence that the building's owner, Emma Sindram, died the very same day.

Seemingly without reason, four days in before Soviet soldiers confiscated the empty lot across the street between Freienwalder Strasse 6–8, Grosse-Leege-Strasse 21–25 and Wriezener Strasse 10–11. Only the plot of land at Freienwalder Strasse 6–7, where the 14th elementary school, destroyed by a direct hit during a bombing on January 20/21, 1944, had stood, remained empty. By early summer it became evident that the soldiers were cultivating vegetables and potatoes on the occupied land.

On October 23, 1948, five staircases of the "Gertruden Courtyard" – a four-story residential complex of the Steglitz non-profit building society at Grosse-Leege-Strasse 17–17a/Schöneicher Strasse 11–11b – was incorporated into the restricted area. 35 apartments had to be evacuated. At about the same time the Soviet occupiers sealed off the Grosse-Leege-Strasse at Wriezener Strasse and the area in front of the entrance to the Kahlbaum spirits factory (No. 97–98). Property numbers 8 and 11 were also blocked off. German civilians were no longer allowed to enter or exit the area.

In 1951 the Ministry of State Security took over the residential buildings in the restricted area. The personal security guards moved with their families into the complex at Grosse-Leege-Strasse 17–17a/Schöneicher Strasse 11–11b. In response to the continually growing staff needs of the State Security Service that was still being built up in the fifties, the leadership decided to create more housing for its staff.

The former "Russian Kohlacker," a coal field at Freienwalder Strasse 6a–8/Grosse-Leege-Strasse 21–25/Wriezener Strasse 10–11, became the center of a large residential housing project in the restricted area. The grounds that were not privately owned stood empty and needed only to be cleared of war debris left behind from the destroyed school. All the necessary work, beginning with the drawing up of architectural sketches to the actual construction measures, was done by inmates of Camp X. To prevent escapes, the compound was enclosed by a tall wooden fence and guard towers.

A residential block with 32 apartments was first erected at Freienwalder Strasse 6–8 in 1953. The next year another 48 apartments were completed at Grosse-Leege-Strasse 21–25. In 1955 the prisoners of the labour camp built two other buildings with forty living units at Freienwalder Strasse 6a–c and Wriezener Strasse 10–11. This complex was expanded from 1955 to 1957 to include an additional thirty apartments on the field of ruins at Freienwalder Strasse 21–23 (which actually belonged to Schöneicher Strasse 8–10) and another eighty apartments at Goeckestrasse 40–42b. On the Goeckestrasse terrain that had once belonged to the Ministry of Aviation Treasury, there was a collection site for military booty that had been run by the Wehrmacht until the end of the war. It was occupied by the Red Army in April 1945 and incorporated into the restricted area at the end of the year.

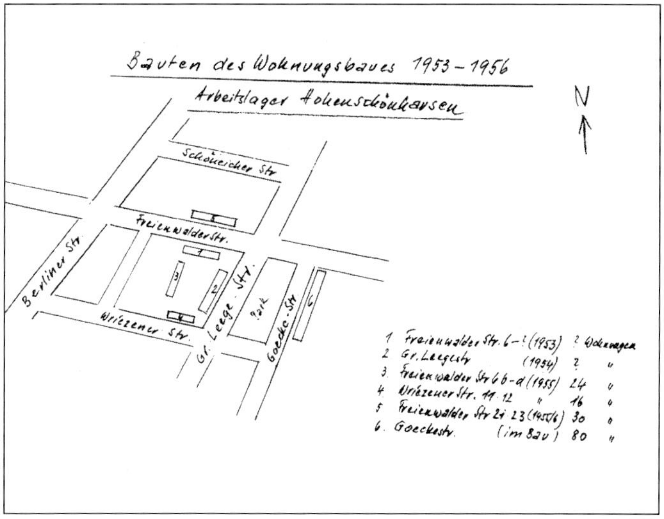

Sketch by an unknown prisoner (1956/57))

Willi Damm, head of Department X and responsible for cooperation with friendly secret services since 1956, was one of the first residents of the "town," as it was called by the population in the State Security Service residential area. Walter Renneberger, head of the driving staff for the Main Department of Administration and Economy, also lived here. Following Minister Mielke's order no. 232/58 from June 30, 1958, a housing administration was established in the Main Department of Administration and Economy. A five-person staff responsible for interior maintenance worked at Freienwalder Strasse 20. At this point at the very latest, the residential blocks were removed from the restricted area, but they continued to bear the status of a "closed residential complex" well into the sixties.

In early 1990 all State Security Service residential property was handed over to the Municipal Residential Administration (KWV). This act was a signal to the population that the omnipotence of the MfS was finally broken and the restricted area would soon be dissolved.

Appendix

Index of Persons

Abbreviations

AfNS	Agency for National Security
BCD	Armaments Department/Chemical Services Department
BStU	Federal Commission for the Records of the State Security Service of the former German Democratic Republic
HAL	Prison Labour Camp
HKH	Central Prison Hospital
HO	Trade Organization
HV A	Main Administration for Reconnaissance
IM	unofficial informers
KRW	Vehicle Repair Shop
LAB	Berlin State Archive
MfS	Ministry of State Security
MGB	Soviet Ministry of State Security
MWD	Soviet Ministry of Internal Affairs
NKGB	Soviet People's Commissariat of State Security
NKVD	Soviet People's Commissariat of Internal Affairs
NSV	National Socialist People's Welfare Organization
OibE	officer in special deployment
OPK	operative identity check
OTS	Operative Technical Sector
OV	operative procedures
PS	Main Department of Personal Security
SBZ	Soviet zone of occupation
SED	Socialist Unity Party of Germany
SCC	Soviet Control Commission
SMAD	Soviet Military Administration in Germany
SSR	Soviet Socialist Republic
UHA	Central Remand Prison
VD	Supply Service
VEB	state-owned company
VRD	Department of Behind the Lines Services
WR	Guard Regiment
ZMD	Central Medical Service

Literature

Askan, Katrin: Aus dem Schneider. Berlin 2000.

ASTAK e. V. Berlin (Hrsg.): Die Zentrale. Das Hauptquartier des Ministeriums für Staatssicherheit in Berlin-Lichtenberg. Berlin o. J.

Bath, Matthias: Gefangen und freigetauscht. 1197 Tage als Fluchthelfer in DDR-Haft. Berlin 2007.

Baumann, Ulrich/Kury, Helmut (Hrsg.): Politisch motivierte Verfolgung: Opfer von SED-Unrecht. Freiburg i.Br. 1998.

Beleites, Johannes: Abteilung XIV: Haftvollzug. MfS-Handbuch, Teil III/9. Herausgegeben von Siegfried Suckut, Ehrhart Neubert, Walter Süß, Roger Engelmann, Bernd Eisenfeld, Jens Giesecke. Berlin 2004.

Beleites, Johannes: Schwerin, Demmlerplatz. Die Untersuchungshaftanstalt des Ministeriums für Staatssicherheit in Schwerin. Hrsg. vom Landesbeauftr. für Mecklenburg-Vorpommern für die Unterlagen des Staatssicherheitsdienstes der ehemal. DDR in Zusammenarbeit mit der Bundesbeauftr. für die Unterlagen des Staatssicherheitsdienstes der ehem. DDR. Schwerin 2001.

Berner, Kurt: Spezialisten hinter Stacheldraht. Ein ostdeutscher Physiker enthüllt die Wahrheit. Berlin 1990.

Bundesinnenministerium der Justiz (Hrsg.): Im Namen des Volkes? Über die Justiz im Staat der SED, 3 Bände. Leipzig 1996.

Crüger, Herbert: Verschwiegene Zeiten. Vom geheimen Apparat der KPD ins Gefängnis der Staatssicherheit. Berlin 1990.

Engelmann, Roger/Vollnhals, Clemens (Hrsg.): Justiz im Dienste der Parteiherrschaft. Rechtspraxis und Staats sicherheit in der DDR. Berlin 2000.

Erler, Peter: Polizeimajor Karl Heinrich – NS-Gegner und Antikommunist. Eine biographische Skizze. Berlin 2007.

Erler, Peter: Sowjetische Geheimdienststrukturen im Industriegebiet Berlin-Hohenschönhausen (Mai 1945 bis Frühjahr 1951). Zur Vorgeschichte, Entwicklung und Topographie des Sperrgebietes Freienwalder Straße/Genslerstraße (Beiträge, Quellen und Materialien zur Diktaturgeschichte, Bd.1/2004). Herausgegeben von der Stiftung Gedenkstätte Berlin-Hohenschönhausen.

Erler, Peter: „Lager X". Das geheime Haftarbeitslager des MfS in Berlin-Hohenschönhausen (1952–1972). Fakten – Dokumente – Personen, Arbeitspapier des Forschungsverbundes SED-Staat Nr. 25/1997. Berlin 1997.

Erler, Peter/Friedrich, Thomas: Das sowjetische Speziallager Nr. 3 Berlin-Hohenschönhausen (Mai 1945 bis Oktober 1946). Herausgegeben vom Verein „Biographische Forschungen und Sozialgeschichte e.V." in Zusammenarbeit mit dem Heimatmuseum Berlin-Hohenschönhausen. Berlin 1995.

Erler, Peter/Friedrich, Thomas (Hrsg.): Genslerstraße 66, Heft 1. Berlin 1995.

Ernst, Ewald: Ein guter Kampf. Fakten, Daten, Erinnerungen. 1945–1954. Sankt Augustin 1998.

Fichter, Horst: Verflucht sei die Menschenwürde. Erlebnisse aus den Zuchthäusern der ehemaligen DDR. Frankfurt/Main 1996.

Flocken, Jan von/Klonovsky, Michael: Stalins Lager in Deutschland 1945–1950. Dokumentation – Zeugenberichte. Berlin/Frankfurt am Main 1991.

Flocken, Jan von/Scholz, Michael F.: Ernst Wollweber. Saboteur – Minister – Unperson. Berlin 1994.

Fricke, Karl Wilhelm: Die DDR-Staatssicherheit. Entwicklung. Strukturen. Aktionsfelder. Köln 1989.

Fricke, Karl Wilhelm/Engelmann, Roger: „Konzentrierte Schläge". Staatssicherheitsaktionen und politische Prozesse in der DDR 1953–1956. Berlin 1998.

Fricke, Karl Wilhelm: Akten-Einsicht. Rekonstruktion einer politischen

Verfolgung. Mit einem Vorwort von Joachim Gauck. Berlin 1995.
Furian, Gilbert: Mehl aus Mielkes Mühlen. Schicksale politisch Verurteilter. Berichte, Briefe, Dokumente. Berlin 1991.
Gedenkstätte Berlin-Hohenschönhausen (Hrsg.): Zeitzeugen – Inhaftiert in Berlin-Hohenschönhausen. Erinnerungen, Protokolle und Fotos zur ehemaligen Lager- und Haftanstalt Berlin-Hohenschönhausen. 4. Auflage 1999.
Gerstner, Karl-Heinz: Sachlich, kritisch und optimistisch. Eine sonntägliche Lebensbetrachtung. Berlin 1999.
Gieseke, Jens: Wer war wer im Ministerium für Staatssicherheit. Kurzbiographien des MfS-Leitungspersonals 1950 bis 1989 (MfS-Handbuch, Teil V/4. Hrsg. von Siegfried Suckut, Ehrhart Neubert, Clemens Vollnhals, Walter Süß, Roger Engelmann). Berlin 1998.
Gieseke, Jens / Hubert, Doris: Die DDR-Staatssicherheit. Schild und Schwert der Partei. Bonn 2000.
Graul, Elisabeth: Die Farce. Ein Stück Autobiographie. 2. korrigierte Auflage, Magdeburg 1995.
Haase, Norbert/Müller, Klaus-Dieter (Hrsg.): Wege nach Bautzen II. Biographische und autobiographische Porträts. Dresden 1998.
Huschner, Anke: Hohenschönhausen (Geschichte der Berliner Verwaltungsbezirke. Herausgegeben von Wolfgang Ribbe, Bd. 15: Hohenschönhausen). Berlin 1995.
Janka, Walter: Schwierigkeiten mit der Wahrheit. Berlin/Weimar 1990.
Kießling, Wolfgang: Partner im „Narrenparadies“. Der Freundeskreis um Noel Field und Paul Merker. Berlin 1994.
Kießling, Wolfgang: Der Fall Baender. Ein Politkrimmi aus den 50er Jahren der DDR. Berlin 1991.
Klein, Manfred: Jugend zwischen den Diktaturen 1945/56. Mainz 1968.
Knabe, Hubertus: Die Täter sind unter uns. Über das Schönreden der SED-Diktatur. Berlin 2007.
Knabe, Hubertus: Die unterwanderte Republik. Stasi im Westen. Berlin 1999.
Knabe, Hubertus: Der diskrete Charme der DDR. Stasi und Westmedien. Berlin 2001.
Kockrow, Wolfgang: „Nicht schuldig!“ Der Versuch einer Aufarbeitung von 51/2 Jahren Zuchthaus in der DDR. Berlin 1999.
Kordon, Klaus: Krokodil im Nacken. Roman. Weinheim, Basel, Berlin 2002.
Kubina, Michael: Von Utopie, Widerstand und Kaltem Krieg. Das unzeitgemäße Leben des Berliner Rätekommunisten Alfred Weiland (1906–1978). Hamburg 2000.
Lang, Jochen von: Erich Mielke. Eine deutsche Karriere. Unter Mitarbeit von Claus Sibyll. Berlin 1991.
Mampel, Siegfried: Entführungsfall Dr. Walter Linse – Menschenraub und Justizmord als Mittel des Staatsterrors (Schriftenreihe des Berliner Landesbeauftragten für die Stasi-Unterlagen, Bd. 10). Berlin 1998.
Matz-Donath, Annerose: Die Spur der roten Spinx. Deutsche Frauen vor sowjetischen Militärtribunalen. Schnellbach 2000.
Otto, Wilfriede: Erich Mielke – Biographie. Aufstieg und Fall eines Tschekisten. Berlin 2000.
Pritzkow, Walter: Sonderlager Nr. 7 – Sachsenhausen. Tatsachenbericht eines Überlebenden aus GPU-Kellern und Sowjet-KZ vom 25. Juni 1945 bis 6. August 1948. Jever 1994.
Raschka, Johannes: Zwischen Überwachung und Repression – Politische Verfolgung in der DDR 1971 bis 1989. Opladen 2001.
Richter, Holger: Die operative Psychologie des Ministeriums für Staatssicherheit der DDR. Frankfurt am Main 2000.
Rieke, Dieter: Geliebtes Leben. Erlebtes und Ertragenes zwischen den Mahlsteinen jüngster deutscher Geschichte. Mit einem Geleitwort von Hans-Jochen Vogel. Berlin 1999.
Scheer, Udo: Jürgen Fuchs. Ein literarischer Weg in die Opposition. Berlin 2008.
Schendzielorz, Gerda: Der Garten der Einsamkeit. Hameln 1995.
Schulze, Hans-Michael: In den Villen der Agenten. Die Stasi-Prominenz privat. Berlin 2003.
Schwan, Heribert: Erich Mielke. Der Mann der die Stasi war. München 1997.

Illustrations

Archiv der sozialen Demokratie, Bonn: 93
Bauarchiv Lichtenberg: 22, 23, 25, 55, 57
Bundesarchiv Koblenz: 35, 72, 80
Bundesbeauftragte für die Stasi-Unterlagen: 9, 11, 12, 13, 14, 15, 16, 17, 20, 38, 39, 40, 41, 42, 45, 50 o., 50 u. (Andreas Schmidt), 52, 63 o., 63 u. li., 64 o., 68, 70, 82, 86, 89 o.
Gedenkstätte Berlin-Hohenschönhausen: 8, 10, 33, 34, 43, 47, 53, 58, 74, 75, 78, 79, 84, 87, 88 u., 89 u., 90, 91, 92
Landesarchiv Berlin: 19, 36, 44, 46, 59, 60, 61, 62, 63 u.re., 64 u., 66, 88 o.
Spiegel, Der, 25. August 1954: 85
Staatliches Archiv der russischen Föderation, Moskau: 27
Stern, 1. Oktober 1950: 30
VEB Tourist Verlag 1984, Buchplan Berlin (on a scale of approx. 1:25 000): 5